D1635663

Brain Map for MRCEM OSCE

Part 1: Communication stations (History taking, Psychiatry and Miscellaneous communication approaches)

Ahmed Hassan

M.B.B.Ch (EGYPT), MRCEM (UK)

BMA LIBRARY
WITHDRAWN LIBRARY
BRITISH MEDICAL ASSOCIATION

WITHDRAWN FROM LIBRARY
BRITISH MEDICAL ASSOCIATION

1000156

PREFACE

Few days before my MRCEM OSCE exam I wrote some notes for my final revision study then I kept reading and practicing and every day I was editing; adding or deleting.

Now after passing MRCEM I would like to share it to help other A&E doctors preparing for this exam.

This book is not a text or a reference; it is just the last minute brain organization before the exam.

It is an extract of a long study of the available books in market, group studies, face to face and online courses and videos.

This book covers history taking, psychiatry and other miscellaneous communication stations.

I will publish another part of this brain map soon to cover examination, procedures and resuscitation stations.

I wish the best for all A&E doctors who will sit this exam in the future hoping that this book would benefit them.

Ahmed Hassan
M.B.B.Ch, MRCEM

TABLE OF CONTENTS

Chapter 1

Psychiatric and self harm assessment approach

The general approach

Setting:
* Appropriate room: calm and easy exit
* Chaperon/security

Introduction:
* Wash hands
* Introduce yourself
* Identify the patient
* Consent (to talk about thoughts)
* How old are you? (Age <19 or >45 are at risk of Suicide in case of depression)
* What do you do for living? (? Financial problems)(? Policeman holding a gun might kill somebody if he has psychiatric illness)

Presenting compliant:
* Start with open question: How are you feeling? Or what's brought you in today? Or who brought you and why?
* Listen as long as appropriate
* Offer pain killer if appropriate
* Check patient understanding why he/she is here if appropriate: What do you know so far about situation?
* Explain situation if appropriate: for example there is a common station in which the patient referred from OPD as he is refusing to take his regular medications at home and he is threatening that he will throw himself out of a running train, so the patient referred to ED for Psychiatric assessment; confirming this data with the patient is a good start of this station
* Offer to see triage observations if appropriate: vital signs, glucose level, oxygen saturation and any signs of injuries especially head injuries

History of presenting complaint:
Nature and characters of the complaint:
* This is appropriate for complaints like hopelessness or strange behaviours.
* You have to ask about ODPARA:
Onset – When did it start, and was it sudden or gradual?
Duration – When was the last time you felt well? Or simply when did it start?
Progression – Was it progressive, regressive or constant?
Aggravating factors, Relieving factors – Anything make it worse or better?
Associated symptoms – Any other associated symptoms?

Overdose:

What? When? How much? Single or Staggered? Other Drugs/Alcohol ingested? Why? Patient's weight? Pregnant or not? (Pregnancy is not CI of most of overdose treatments) Previous similar attempts? Organized attempt? (Any precautions taken against discovery – who discovered you and how? Any attempts to get help? Any in advance preparations undertaken like suicide notes or closing bank account?)

Mood:

Explore either low or high mood by asking:

* How have you been feeling in yourself?
* Ask about biological symptoms of depression: sleep, appetite and libido
* Ask about anhedonia: are you still get enjoyment from doing things used to enjoy?
* Ask about suicidal ideation or attempts and explore the stated future intent

Thoughts:

Explore rational thinking loss by asking:

* Tell me about your thoughts?
* Do you have particular things in your mind? (preoccupation)
* Do you have beliefs that others disagree about? Do you believe that some people against you, something strange going on or interfered with by person or outside force? (Delusions)

Perception/hallucinations:

Have you ever seen or heard things that other people couldn't?

Insight:

Do you think there is something wrong with you? Do you think that you need treatment? If yes, What is it?

Cognition:

Usually not needed in details if not requested clearly; ask the first couple of questions and if you find it abnormal try to complete it if time allows

Mini Mental State Examination:

Explain to patient that you need to ask them a series of questions, some of which will be very easy and some of which may be harder.

Mnemonic: ORArL 2,3 RWD

Orientation (10):

> * Day, date, month, year, season
> * Floor, building, town/city, county, country

Registration (3): ask patient to repeat "ball, car, man" and tell patient to remember them and you will ask them again later

Attention (5): spell "world" backwards

Recall (3): repeat the 3 wards

Language (1): repeat "no ifs and or buts"

2 – Name 2 objects (2): pen, cup

3 – 3 stage command (3): take this paper, fold it in half and put it on the floor

Reading (1): write on paper "close your eyes" and ask patient to follow instruction
Writing (1): ask patient to write a short sentence
Drawing (1): ask patient to copy drawing shown

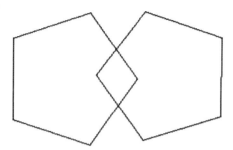

Scoring: > 24 normal, 16-24 mild impairment and <16 severe impairment

Past medical, surgical and psychiatric history:

* Epilepsy, dementia or other neurological problems
* Liver disease, eating disorders or malnutrition: low threshold for paracetamol toxicity
* Psychiatric illness, previous hospital admission either voluntary or compulsory and previous outpatient contact like CPN or day centers

MAFTOS (Medications, Allergies, Family history, Travel history, Social history):

Medications and allergies:

* List of medications and compliance
* Special attention to anticonvulsants, rifampicin or St John's wart use in case of paracetamol overdose as it all reduces the threshold of paracetamol toxicity

Family history:

* Life history: education, family and friends
* Explore the social support either positive or negative

Social history:

* Relationship history and current partner
* Smoking, alcohol and illicit drugs history
* Explore either the patient is single or not and use excess alcohol and illicit drugs or not

Closing:

Summarize findings for examples:

* Findings of Mental State Examination (MSE)
* Findings of Drug Overdose history taking
* Findings of Suicide risk assessment
* Findings of Capacity assessment

Plan further care:

According to the findings

Examples from previous exams

Mental State Examination (MSE) station

Comment on:

1- Appearance and behaviour:

* Appearance: dress and posture

* Activity: still or fidgeting

* Social & emotional: apathy, irritable or tearful

2- Speech:

* Fast (pressure): mania

* Slow (tailing off): depression

3- Mood: high or low

4- Thoughts: preoccupation, delusions

5- perception: hallucinations

6- Insight: preserved or not

7- Cognition: normal or impaired

Urosepsis MSE station:

In this station the examiner will ask you to do mental state examination; follow the general approach but take your time doing mini-mental state examination in details then:

Summarize findings, for example:

Impairment of cognitive function, probably due to UTI

Plan further care, for example:

* Monitor

* Vital signs

* Examination: general and local

* Put IV cannula and extract blood

* Take urine sample for analysis and culture

* Give IV fluids and IV antibiotics

* Admit the patient to the medical ward

Mania MSE station:

In this station the examiner will ask you to do mental state examination; follow the general approach and ask only couple of questions in mini-mental state examination then:

Summarize findings, for example:

* Well dressed, active and irritable

* Fast speech

* High mood and no suicidal ideation

* Preoccupation and delusions

* No hallucination

* Lack of insight

* Preserved cognitive function

Plan further care, for example:
* Investigations to rule out organic/medical cause of a psychiatric presentation
* Psychiatric referral if indicated

Drug overdose history taking station

In this station the examiner will ask you to take history from a patient or a junior doctor then to discuss management plan with the patient, junior doctor or the examiner. Sometimes the examiner will tell you that basic blood investigations extracted, so you have to ask about results at the end as it will likely affect your management plan. At the beginning of this station you have to confirm patient's stability and safety by confirming normal observations and vital signs. If you are taking the history from a junior doctor confirm that somebody taking care of the patient and that the patient is placed in a monitored area. Follow the general approach with concentration on medical history and medical treatment rather than concentration on psychiatric assessment then:
Summarize findings by recalling the important points in the history including the toxic dose of the ingested drug, for example:
1- In case of paracetamol overdose:
State that the patient received a toxic dose of paracetamol (12g or 150mg/kg for low risk patients) or (6g or 75mg/kg for high risk patients)
2- In case of iron overdose:
This patient received a toxic dose of elemental iron (>60mg/kg)
3- In case of TCA overdose:
This patient received toxic dose of TCA 15mg/kg
Plan further care, for example:
1- In case of paracetamol overdose:
* Activated charcoal within one hour
* 4 hours blood paracetamol level
* Interpreting the drug levels against the treatment nomogram
* Treat with NAC or an alternative (methionine)
* Thiamine (oral or parenteral) for possible thiamine deficiency in case of chronic alcoholism
* Inpatient detoxification for alcohol withdrawal
* Ask about blood test results, identify risk to liver and inform the patient clearly that he might lose his liver
* Consult liver team if indicated: coagulopathy, acidosis, renal impairment or encephalopathy
2- In case of iron overdose:
* Gastric lavage if >20mg/kg elemental iron has been taken within one hour and whole bowel irrigation may be useful if many tablets remain in gut evidenced by plain abdominal X ray film and this is the case in the slow release formulations
* 4 hours blood iron level
* Interpret iron level result as sever toxicity if it is >5mg/L

* Treat with desferroxamine in serious toxicity as indicated with coma or shock; dose is 15mg/kg/hr IV infusion with maximum dose of 80mg/kg in 24 hours. It may cause hypotension or rash if infused rapidly. Rarely it might cause anaphylaxis, pulmonary oedema or ARDS. Reduce dose with clinical improvement.
* Ask about blood test results and identify risk to liver and kidney; iron toxicity can cause acidosis, coagulopathy, renal failure and hepatic failure.

3- In case of TCA overdose:
* Activated charcoal up to 2 hours after ingestion because TCA cause delayed gastric emptying
* Sodium bicarbonate: if QRS>120ms or arrhythmias in ECG, hypotension not responded to IV fluids or metabolic acidosis in ABG. Give dose of 50mmol (50ml of 8.4%) and repeat it till PH 7.50-7.55 and QRS<100ms
* Benzodiazepine for seizures
N.B: TOXBASE should be consulted if needed and capacity should be assessed if requested or if the patient refused treatment

Suicide risk assessment (SAD PERSONS score) station

In this station the examiner will ask you to do suicide risk assessment usually with capacity assessment even if not clearly requested. Follow the general approach then summarize the findings and plan further care accordingly

SAD PERSONS score:
Sex: male scores **1**
Age: <19, >45 years scores **1**
Depression or hopelessness: scores **2**
Previous suicide attempt/psychiatric care: scores **1**
Excess alcohol or drug use: scores **1**
Rational thought loss: scores **2**
Separated, widowed or divorced: scores **1**
Organized or serious attempt: scores **2**
No social support: scores **1**
Stated future intent: scores **2**
Scoring: <6 (may be safe to discharge depending upon circumstances), 6-8 (probably warrants a psychiatric assessment) and >8 (probably requires hospital admission)

Capacity assessment station

In this station the examiner will ask you to assess capacity or you will do it as a part of the full psychiatric interview. Assess it if clearly requested in the question or if the patient is refusing treatment (for example NAC for paracetamol overdose or desferroxamine for iron overdose). After capacity assessment summarize findings and state either that the patient has capacity or not then plan further care accordingly. As a general rule you can't force a patient with full capacity to stay in the hospital for treatment.

Capacity assessment technique:
* Explore concerns
* Empathize
* Attempt to persuade: give information about the treatment, need and benefits as well as risks of treating and not treating the condition and finally alternatives to treatment; pros and cons of each alternative comparing it to the recommended treatment
* Try to involve relatives
* Check understanding: give time for reflection and tell the patient that he has the right to change his mind at any stage
* Check retaining
* Check that patient weighs benefits and risks of the decision (for example refusing a treatment)
* Check that patient communicate decision clearly

Chapter 2

Brief intervention of alcohol approach

Introduction:
* Introduce yourself
* Identify the patient
* Consent
* How old are you?
* What do you do for living?

Presenting complaint:
* Check patient understanding why he is here: what do you know so far about your situation?
* Explain situation and tell the patient that you are going to do screen for heavy drinking

History of presenting complaint:

Assess alcohol use:
* Do you sometimes drink beer, wine or other alcoholic beverages?
* How many times in the past year have you had 5 (for men) or 4 (for women) drinks in a day? If the answer is one or more it means that the patient is at risk drinker
* On average, how many days a week do you have an alcoholic drink?
* On a typical drinking day, how many drinks dou you have?

Assess for alcohol use disorders:
* In the past year did your drinking repeateadly cause:
1- Risk of serious bodily harm (during driving or swimming)
2- Relationship troubles (family or friends)
3- Role failure (interferance with home or work obligations)
4- Run-ins with law (arrest)
If the answer is yes for one or more of the previous questions it means that the patient's drinking habits put him under category of alcohol abuse
* In the past year are you:
1- Not able to stick to drinking limits
2- Not been able to cut down or stop drinking
3- Shown tolerance (needed to drink a lot more to get the same effect)
4- Shown signs of withdrwal (tremors, sweating, nausea, insomnia when you trying to quite or cut down drinking)
5- Kept drinking despite physical or psychological problems
6- Spent lot of time drinking
7- Spent less time on other important or pleasurable matters
If the answer is yes for three or more of the previous questions it means that the patient's drinking habits put him under category of alcohol dependance

Past medical, surgical and psychiatric history:

* Alcohol related medical problems
* Psychiatric history of previous illness/diagnosis, previous hospitalization either voluntary or compulsory and outpatient contact either CPN (Community Psychiatric Nurse) or day centers

MAFTOS (Medications, Allergies, Family history, Travel history, Social history):

* Medications and allergies: list of medications and compliance
* Family history: life history including education, family and friends
* Social history: smoking and illicit drugs

Closing:

State conclusion:

Tell the patient clearly that his drinking habits put him under category of at risk drinker or alcohol abuse disorders (abuse or dependence)

State recommendation:

Limit your drinks to 4 per day or 14 per week for men and 3 per day or 7 per week for women

Check readiness to change drinking habits:

* *If patient is ready to change drinking habits:*
1- Help set a goal (limit or stop drinking)
2- Agree a plan
3- Provide patient with educational materials
4- For alcohol use disorders; consider evaluation by addiction specialist and recommend help groups
5- For alcohol dependence; consider detoxification if stopping drinking is the goal
6- Document alcohol use and review goals at each visit to ED or arrange GP follow up

* *If patient is not ready to change drinking habits:*
1- Restate your concern
2- Encourage reflection
3- Address barriers to change
4- Reaffirm your willingness to help

Chapter 3

Confusion assessment approach

Introduction:

Nurse:
* Introduce yourself
* Identify the nurse
* Identify the nurse's role

Patient:
* Wash your hands
* Introduce yourself
* Identify the patient
* Consent
* Confirm confusion: attempt MMSE; ask couple of questions only
* Ask for clues: handover, collateral history (relatives, GP and hospital notes) and look for bracelet
* Rapid assessment of ABCDE
* Baseline observations especially temperature and SPO2
* Assess for head injury
* Take bedside blood sugar
* Identify hypoglycemia (RBS < 3mmol/L) and treat it: oral juice/sweet, IM/SC glucagon or IV dextrose 10% 50ml and repeat every 2 minutes until recovery or 250ml has been given
* Request blood gas analysis
* Identify hyperkalemia and hyponatremia and give IV fluids and IV hydrocortisone 100mg
* Ensures back to normal
* Reintroduce yourself and the nurse to the patient
* Re-identify the patient
* Re-consent to talk to the patient
* How old are you?
* What do you do for living?

Presenting complaint:
* How are you feeling?
* What's brought you in today? Who brought you in today? Why?
* Offer pain killer if appropriate
* Check patient understanding of the situation: what do you know so far about your condition?
* Explain the situation: events till now

History of presenting complaint:
* What do you remember of the event if anything?
* ODPARA: mnemonic for main complaint analysis
* Systemic review looking for the cause/precipitation of the confusion state:
- Systemic: fever
- Urinary: dysuria, haematuria or frequency
- GI: vomiting, diarrhoea or abdominal pain
- Fall or head injury
- Events before confusion: celebration/drinking binge, undue exercise, delayed food intake, missed or excess medicine
* Previous similar episodes

Past medical and surgical history and previous hospitalization:
* Diabetes mellitus; ask about hypoglycemia awareness
* Addison's disease
* Chronic renal failure
* Chronic liver failure
* Hypo/hyperthyroidism
* Epilepsy
* Malignancy
* Recent surgery

MAFTOS (Medications, Allergies, Family history, Travel history, Social history):
Medications and allergies:
* Insulin, oral hypoglycaemic, steroids, benzodiazepines, opioids, anticonvulsants or anti-parkinsonism
* Confirm missed food after taking insulin in case of confusion due to hypoglycaemia
* Confirm missed steroids in case of confusion due to adrenal insufficiency

Social history:
* Family support: who lives with you? Who takes care of you?
* Smoking, alcohol (dependence) or illicit drugs

Closing:
Anything else you feel I should know

Examination:
Explain that you might need to examine him/her (in case of adrenal insufficiency)

Laboratory tests:
Explain that you might need to request some blood and or urine tests (in case of adrenal insufficiency)

DD and likely diagnosis (examples from previous exams):
* Hypoglycemia due to missed meal after injecting insulin/eating oral hypoglycemic, increased insulin dose by GP recently or oral hypoglycemic overdose
* Adrenal insufficiency due to missed steroid and stress from concurrent illness (gastritis, pancreatitis, infection ... etc)

What we will do now:

Hypoglycemia:

* Discharge:

Discharge patient who recovers completely after short acting insulin induced hypoglycaemia after a couple of hours of observation with the following instructions:

1- Return to previous insulin dose if the dose is increased recently

2- Advice regarding balanced food and not forget to eat after insulin injection or oral hypoglycaemic ingestion

3- Advice regarding importance of exercise but warn of risk of hypoglycaemia from undue exercise

4- Discharge with written instruction/leaflets and GP follow up

* Admission:

Admit patient with oral hypoglycemic-induced hypoglycemia or long acting insulin induced hypoglycemia

Adrenal insufficiency:

* Usually needs admission for steroids, IV fluids, dextrose, anti-emetics and management of infection

* Advice to continue steroids, not to stop it suddenly and to increase the dose at time of stress (trauma, infection, surgery or acute illness)

General instructions:

1- Explain the importance of bracelet

2- Explain the importance of family support

3- Explain the importance of awareness of neighbours/relatives of patient's condition and what should patient or accompaniers do in case of emergency

4- Advice regarding alcohol intake

Chapter 4

Teach an interpretation of a test or a medication use approach

The general approach

Introduction:
* Introduce yourself
* Identify the student/junior doctor (name, grade, skills)
* Confirm the task
* List the objectives

Patient:

Safety:

Where is the patient? Is patient's in resuscitation/monitored area? How are patient's vitals? Anybody take care of patient?

Review indication and contraindication of test or medication:

Ask about brief history, examination and investigations findings to answer the question why this test or medication needed and to ensure that there is no contraindication or another more suitable option

Consent:

Discuss possible side effects with the patient

Paper or radiograph tests:
* Patient's details: name and DOB
* Date and time: ask about serial or previous studies
* Type of the test

Approach

Post test or treatment
* Post test: diagnosis and treatment
* Post treatment: disposition and plan

Closing:
* Check understanding
* Allow student/junior doctor to ask questions
* Invite to demonstrate knowledge/attempt the task
* Correct when a mistake is made without being patronizing
* Offer to review the patient
* Establishes future learning goals

Blood gas analysis

Review indication:
Respiratory and metabolic
Type:
Venous or arterial sample on room air or ?FiO2
Approach:
5 steps approach
1- How is the patient?
Predict the effect of the pathological process on the blood gas e.g.
sepsis and DKA → metabolic acidosis (low pH, low HCO3) →
hyperventilation and respiratory compensation (low PCO2); all these
findings could be associated with normal or impaired oxygenation. If
PCO2 is high → hypoventilation (associated low conscious level or acute
respiratory illness)
2- Assess oxygenation:
 PaO2 should be >10KPa on air and about 10KPa<FiO2 (1KPa is about
7.5mmgh)
3- Determine pH:
<7.35 → acidosis and >7.45 → alkalosis
4- Determine respiratory component (PCO2):
* >6KPa or 45mmgh → either respiratory acidosis or respiratory
compensation of metabolic alkalosis
* <4.7KPa or 35mmgh → either respiratory alkalosis or respiratory
compensation of metabolic acidosis
5- Determine metabolic component (HCO3):
* <22mmol/L → either metabolic acidosis or renal compensation of
respiratory alkalosis
* >26mmol/L → either metabolic alkalosis or renal compensation of
respiratory acidosis
* Base deficit <-2 is a mirror of HCO3 <22mmol/L
* Base excess >+2 is a mirror of HCO3 >26mmol/L
Diagnosis:
Example from previous exam (patient with DKA and pneumonia Ph 7.22,
PO2 55, PCO2 60 and HCO3 15):
1- Primary disturbance: metabolic acidosis
2- Degree of compensation or mixed component: no respiratory
compensation → respiratory acidosis from hypoventilation either due
to low conscious level or extensive ARDS)
3- Impaired oxygenation
Treatment:
Example from previous exam (patient with DKA and pneumonia Ph 7.22,
PO2 55, PCO2 60, HCO3 15):

Call for help:

Call for help: from either rapid response team, critical care outreach team or medical/ITU team

Sepsis 6:

1- Oxygenation or intubation with ventilator settings of low tidal volume (permissive hypercapnoea)

2- IV fluids

3- IFC: UOP monitoring to keep it >0.5ml/kg/hr

4- Blood culture

5- Serum lactate

6- Antibiotics

ECG interpretation

Review indication:

Cardiac and non-cardiac

Type:

* 12 lead ECG with rhythm strip

* Speed 25mm/sec → small square = 0.04 sec, large square = 0.2 sec and 5 large squares = 1 sec

* Deflection of 10mm = 1mv

Approach:

6 stages approach:

1- Any electrical activity?

2- What is the ventricular (QRS) rate?

* Number of large squares in one R-R interval/300 or

* Number of small squares in R-R interval/1500 or

* Number of R waves in 10 seconds X 6

3- Is QRS rhythm regular or irregular?

If irregular → A fib, premature contractions or heart block

4- Is QRS width normal or abnormal?

* Normal <0.12sec → normal or SVT

* Wide >0.12sec → BBB or VT

5- Is atrial activity present (P wave)? If present what character?

* If absent → A fib, SVT or hyperkalemia

* Character of normal P wave: width 0.12sec and height 2.5mm

6- Is atrial activity (P wave) related to ventricular activity (QRS complex)? And how?

* Every P wave followed by QRS complex → either normal sinus rhythm, WPW syndrome (short PR interval <0.12sec, delta wave and wide QRS) or first degree heart block (PR interval: prolonged >0.2sec)

* P wave coming after QRS complex → junctional rhythm

* Some P wave without QRS complexes→ either mobitz I (increasingly lengthened PR interval until P failed to conduct), mobitz II (2:1, 3:1 block... etc) or escape rhythm in CHB (no relation between P waves and QRS)

Comment on the following if appropriate:

QRS amplitude:
LVH → SV2 + RV5 >35mm, R I >15mm or R AVL >11mm
QT interval:
QTc = QT/square root R-R interval; normal value <0.44 sec
Axis:
* Normal → leads I and II has positive QRS deflection
* Left axis deviation → lead I have positive QRS deflection while it is negative in leads II and AVF
* Right axis deviation → lead I has negative QRS deflection while it is positive in leads II and AVF
Ischemic changes:
* Pathological Q wave: if width >0.04sec or depth >1/2 height of subsequent R wave
* ST elevation: caused by either acute MI, pericarditis, ventricular aneurysm, prinzmetal's angina, LVH, Brugada syndrome or benign early repolarisation

MI territory (area involved)	ECG leads showing ST elevation	ECG leads showing reciprocal changes	Artery involved
Septal	V1-2	None	Left anterior descending (LAD)
Anterior (left ventricle)	V3-4	I, avl	LAD
Antero-septal (septum and left ventricle)	V1-4	I, avl	LAD
Antero-lateral (left ventricle)	I, avl, V3-6	II, III, avf	LAD or circumflex
Inferior (left ventricle and apex)	II, III, avf	I, avl	Right coronary artery
Posterior (posterior wall of left ventricle)	V7-9	Tall R waves and ST depression V1-3	Right coronary artery or circumflex
Right ventricular	II, III, avf, V1, V4R	I, avl	Right coronary artery

* ST depression: ischemia, digoxin or LVH with strain
* Peaked T wave: MI or hyperkalemia
* Flat T wave: ischemia or hypokalemia
* Inverted T wave: ischemia especially V4-6

Diagnosis and treatment:

Examples from previous exams:

1- SVT:

* Stable: vagal maneuvers and adenosine (6-12-12 mg)

* Unstable: cardio-version 70-120 joules biphasic

* WPW: avoid AV blockers and give flecanide to control rate

* Identify and treat the cause of SVT (for example caffeine and drugs)

2- MI:

Treatment of MI is known but be aware of special treatment consideration for RV MI → avoid nitrates, give IV fluids, PCI/thrombolytic and finally don't forget that RV MI has poor prognosis

Chest X ray interpretation

Review indication:

Cardiac, pulmonary, trauma and acute abdomen

Type:

* Antero-posterior or poster-anterior

* Inspiratory or expiratory film

* Standing, sitting or supine film

Approach:

ABCDE approach:

A: Adequacy:

* The film should show lung apices, cost diaphragmatic angle and scapulae should be out of the way

* No rotation if distances from medial end of the clavicle to spinous processes are equal bilaterally

* Adequate penetration if vertebral bodies just visible through the heart

* Adequate inflation if 5-6 ribs anteriorly are visible on inspiratory film

A: Airway:

Tracheal deviation in pneumothorax, effusion, collapse or rotation

B: Breathing:

* Lung fields: describe any abnormality as uniform/non-uniform, bone/soft tissue/fat/air density, in right/left lung, in upper (above 2nd rib anteriorly)/middle (between 2nd and 4th ribs anteriorly)/lower (below 4th rib anteriorly) zone.

* Silhouette sign: obscured diaphragm border → lower lobe opacity and obscured cardiac border → middle lobe opacity in right lung or lingual opacity in left lung

* Hilum: look for lymphadenopathy or pulmonary artery enlargement

C: Circulation:

* Heart size: <1/2 thorax diameter is normal

* Mediastinum size

* Great vessels: look for obliteration of aortic knob and Aorto-pulmonary window

D: Diaphragm:
* Costophrenic angles
* Air below diaphragm
E: Everything else:
* Bones: clavicles, ribs and scapulae
* Soft tissues: surgical emphysema
* Tubes: chest tube, ETT and NGT
Diagnosis and treatment:
* Collapse: uniform soft tissue density
* Consolidation: non uniform soft tissue density with air bronchogram
* Effusion: uniform soft tissue density with meniscus sign
* Pneumothorax: uniform air density lateral to the pleura
* COPD: hyperinflation (>8 ribs are visible anteriorly, flat hemi-diaphragms), decreased lung markings, black lesion (bulla) and prominent hilum
* Pulmonary edema: ABCDE → Alveolar shadowing (bats wings sign), B-lines (interstitial edema), Cardiomegaly, Diversion of blood to upper lobes and Effusion

C spine X ray interpretation

Review indication:
If you can't clear C spine clinically
Review contraindication:
Pan CT or brain CT required for multiple trauma or head injury
Type:
Antero-posterior, lateral and open mouth odontoid peg views
Approach:
ABCDE approach:
A: Adequacy:
The film should show 7 C vertebrae and superior aspect of T1
A: Alignment:
4 lines should align vertically on lateral film: anterior vertebral line, anterior spinal line, posterior spinal line and spinous processes line
B: Bones:
* Vertebrae: look for height preservation and bony cortex integrity
* Facets: look for dislocation
* Spinous processes: look for integrity
C: Cartilage:
Disk spaces: look for narrowing or widening
D: Dens:
Look for outline integrity and the pre-dental space which should be <3mm
E: Extra-axial soft tissue:
* Space at the level of C3 should be <7mm
* Space at the level of C7 should be <3mm

Diagnosis and treatment:
Review spines injury chapter from ATLS

N acetylecysteine (NAC) use

Review indication:
1- <8 hours from paracetamol overdose → if paracetamol blood level above treatment level on nomogram

2- 8 to 24 hours from paracetamol overdose → if potentially toxic paracetamol dose ingested NAC should started immediately then it can be stopped later if paracetamol blood level below treatment level on nomogram and no evidence of liver or renal dysfunction

3- >24 hours from pracetamol overdose → if there is any detectable amount of paracetamol in blood or if there is evidence of liver dysfunction by examination (jaundice or tender liver) or biochemical markers (INR>1.3 or ALT>twice the upper limit of normal)

4- Staggered paracetamol overdose → if patient ingested a potentially toxic paracetamol dose NAC should be started immediately then it can stopped later if no evidence of liver or renal dysfunction 24 hours after the last ingestion

Review contraindication:
Allergy

Consent:
Inform the patient about side effects which could be local (erythema or urticaria) which don't need intervention or systemic (generalized rashes, itching, nausea, angioedema, bronchospasm, hypotension or hypertension) which require stopping treatment, giving antihistamine then resuming treatment at the lowest infusion rate after settling of symptoms

Approach:
* There are two available antidotes for paracetamol toxicity in the UK: acetylcysteine and methionine.

* They work by binding to the toxic metabolite (NAPQI) and preventing hepatic necrosis.

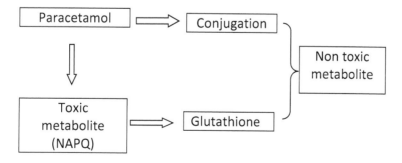

* Acetylcysteine is the most commonly used antidote and is given intravenously. The dosing schedule is:
- 150 mg/kg in 200 ml 5% glucose over 1 hour.
- 50 mg/kg in 500 ml 5% glucose over 4 hours.
- 100 mg/kg in 1000 ml 5 % glucose over 16 hours.
* Methionine is an oral formulation that can be used if intravenous access is not possible.
* TOXBASE now recommends giving the intravenous acetylcysteine formulation orally, instead of methionine, if intravenous access cannot be gained. The dosage of orally acetylcysteine is available on the TOXBASE website

Disposition and plan:
* Reassessment, observation and admission
* Indications of liver transplantation team involvement: as mentioned earlier in chapter 1

Chapter 5

Major incident approach

The general approach

Introduction:
* Introduce yourself
* Identify the nurse (name, grade and skills)
* How can I help you?
METHANE report: given by police or ambulance service:
M: Major incident standby or declared
E: Exact location
T: Type of incident
H: Hazards present and potential
A: Access to scene and egress route
N: Number and severity of casualties
E: Emergency service present or required
Approach
Closing:
* Any question?
* Let's go

Examples from previous exams

On scene triage approach

You suppose to explain the major incident procedure to a junior nurse with no previous experience in "on scene triage"
Arrival at scene:
* We will take with us kit bags which composed of ABC equipments and drugs
* We will wear our PPE (helmet, jacket, gloves, boots, eye and ear protections)
* We should have log, radio and tabard
* We will arrive at scene as MERIT (Medical Emergency Response Incident Team) or MMT (Mobile Medical Team) which contains two members a doctor and a nurse, two doctors or two nurses
* We will report to MIO (Medical Incident Officer) or AIO (Ambulance Incident Officer) and we will identify their location by looking for a flashing green and blue lights respectively
* The scene is divided into bronze area and silver area

* We will either stay in the silver area to make triage and evacuate patients to CCS (Casualty Clearing Station) or go to CCS where resuscitation taking place and from where patients are transferred to the hospital
* We will not be allowed to enter the bronze area where the fire services are working

Triage process:

Sieve:

Patient's status	Priority
Walking and not injured	Survivors reception centre
Walking and injured	Priority 3 (Delayed)
Not walking, no spontaneous breathing and not breathing after opening airway	Dead
Not walking, no spontaneous breathing but breathing after opening airway	Priority 1 (Immediate)
Not walking, spontaneous breathing and respiratory rate (RR) 9 or less / 30 or more	Priority 1 (Immediate)
Not walking, spontaneous breathing, RR 10-29 and pulse rate (PR) over 120 or Capillary Refill Time (CRT) > 2	Priority 1 (Immediate)
Not walking, spontaneous breathing, RR 10-29 and PR under 120 or CRT 2 or less	Priority 2 (Urgent)

Sort:

Step 1: calculate the Glasgow Coma Score (GCS):

A: Eye opening	Score	B: Verbal response	Score	C: Motor response	Score
Spontaneous	4	Oriented	5	Follow command	6
To voice	3	Confused	4	Localize pain	5
To pain	2	Inappropriate	3	Withdrawal to pain	4
None	1	Incomprehensible	2	Flexion to pain	3
		No response	1	Extension to pain	2
				No response	1

GCS = A + B + C

Step 2: Calculate the triage sort score:

X: Convert GCS	Score	Y: Respiratory rate	Score	Z: Systolic blood pressure	Score
13-15	4	10-29	4	90 or more	4
9-12	3	>29	3	76-89	3
6-8	2	6-9	2	50-75	2
4-5	1	1-5	1	1-49	1
3	0	0	0	0	0

Triage sort score = X + Y + Z

Step 3: Assign a triage priority

Triage sort score	Priority status	Priority color
12	3	Green
11	2	Yellow
10 or less	1	Red
0	Dead	Blue or black

Step 4: Upgrade priority dependant on injury/diagnosis

Triage card:
It is a 4 armed card colored red, yellow, green and black (sometimes blue) which are the color codes for priority 1,2,3 and dead victims respectively. The appropriate arm can be displayed to indicate the priority status of the victim, and it could be changed to another color if required as triage is a dynamic process

In hospital preparation and prioritization approach

You suppose to explain the major incident procedure to a junior nurse with no previous experience in "in hospital preparation and prioritization"

Preparation:
* Activate major incident cascade through switchboard
* Inform ED consultant, nurse in charge and all ED staff
* Discuss possibility of calling in off duty staff
* Activate the department major incident plan and use action cards to delegate roles to staff
* Assess and safely clear waiting room and minor area
* Assess and safely transfer major and resuscitation patients to wards
* Set up triage area outside the hospital door
* Reassign ED areas to red, yellow, green and black zones

* Use major incident triage cards and numbers to identify patients either coming from the incident or not
* Request extra security and lock down the ED to prevent media within the ED
* For chemical incident preparation be aware of extra steps:
1- Inform local health protection team
2- Get expert advice from Toxbase
3- Set decontamination area outside the triage area and assign staff for decontamination with full PPE
4- Be aware of possible agents → chlorine, tear gases, cyanide and organophosphate (nerve gas → sarin)
5- Be aware of specific antidotes → hydroxycobalamine for cyanide and atropine/pralidoxime for organophosphates

Prioritization:
* Priority 1 → P1 → Red → Emergency/Immediate → life threatening injuries needs resuscitation; subsequently prioritized according to ABC approach and salvage ability
* Priority 2 → P2 → Yellow → Urgent → serious injuries needs urgent intervention
* Priority 3 → P3 → Green → Non urgent/Delayed → minor or moderate injuries needs simple measures
* Dead → Blue or black

Examples:

Fire incident prioritization:
1- 65 year male with burned/charred face, cough black particles with sputum and asking for water → P1 → inhalation injury → needs early intubation → this patient will take priority over other P1 patients according to ABC approach and salvage ability
2- 40 year with burn over trunk and limbs, BP 80/40, P 120 and sat 86% on high flow oxygen → P1 → shocked → needs oxygen and fluids and needs assessment and management of burn, chest trauma and internal hemorrhage
3- 90 year with second and third degree burn about 70% P 110, BP 130/90 and sat 92% on 4L oxygen → P1 → extensive burn → needs fluid → priority will be given to another patient with better salvage ability
4- 30 year with circumferential both arms burn and in pain → P2 → compartment syndrome → needs escharotomy and morphine → this patient will take priority over other P2 patients as there is a limb threatening injury
5- Young man with scalp bruise and GCS 12, BP 130/85 and P 90 → P2 → moderate head injury → needs CT brain, close observation and management to prevent secondary brain injury
6- Family of 4; mother hold baby, father grumbling and complaint, sister need food to eat and clinically stable → P3
7- 11 residents of the home are sitting on wheel chairs and talking and some of them are asking for blankets because they feel the ED cold → P3

Chemical incident (unknown substance splash) prioritization:

1- Seizure → P1 → needs airway management and diazepam → this patient will take priority over other P1 patients as per ABC approach

2- Breathing difficulty (hypoxia) → P1 → needs oxygen, bronchodilators with possible need for IPPV

3- Red eyes → P2 → needs eye irrigation, flourcein examination and ophthalmology referral → some protocols consider this patient P1 case as there is sight threatening injury but any how airway and breathing concerns has the priority

4- Sore eyes and throat with excessive lacrimation → P3 → needs eye irrigation and observation

Chapter 6

Breaking bad news (BBN) approach

SPIKES BBN protocol

Setting:
* Review ED notes
* Comfortable, confidential room without interruptions; close mobile and bleep
* Accompany senior nurse with you
* Inform in charge nurse where you are
* Introduce your self
* Identify patient or relative and his relation to the patient

Perception:
* What do you know so far about the situation?
* What was his/her previous quality of life?
* Explain situation: recall events till now but don't even touch the bad news; at this stage you can explain clinical and workup findings like CT findings in layman English as well as treatment given, you can offer showing the scan images to the relative for example.

Examples from previous exams:
Haematemesis patient is going to die:
Patient with chronic liver disease, alcoholic and on liver transplantation list presented with non-stop vomiting of blood, blood pressure very low, HB is very low and received many bags of blood
Cardiogenic shock patient is going to die:
Elderly patient with previous heart attacks presented with new heart attack, efforts done to make her/his heart to beat again; now her/his heart is beating but her/his blood pressure is very low and she/he is receiving medicines to raise her/his blood pressure
CA lung patient is going to die:
Patient with no previous illnesses presented unconscious; skull and chest scan showed big C (growth) in her/his lungs and skull piece
ICH patient is going to die:
Patient presented unconscious; skull scan showed skull fracture at the back and blood around the brain which causing pressure on his/her brain

Invitation:
* Would you prefer a family member or a friend to be present?
* Would you like to know how he/she is now?

Knowledge:
I'm sorry to say that I have some bad news for you (pause), sadly Mr./Mrs. ..... is going to die/has died (silence 10sec)

Empathy:

Acknowledge response and treat it appropriately:

* Offer tissue (if crying)

* Say I can't imagine how you feel but I'm sorry (if denying or not believing)

* Say I can see that this news was a huge shock (if she/he is angry)

* Say Can I ask what's going through your mind? (if she/he is silent)

* Say what's upsetting you the most? (if mixed emotions)

Strategy:

Died:

* Guide her/him to bereavement office

* State that coroner might be involved; coroner is usually involved in unexpected deaths

Going to die:

Rational of stating that patient is going to die:

* Fatal/poor prognosis: you can say that the illness is not for intervention or not for surgery or not responded despite aggressive treatment, you can add that the illness caused large, deep, multiple and extensive damage in case of ICH or brain metastasis for example

* State that the specialty team involved in the decision e.g. ITU, cardiology, neurosurgery, trauma team, pediatric team, liver team ... etc

Plan:

* We will keep her/him in a comfortable room, put her/him on oxygen and give her/him fluids and pain killers

* Explain that decision is not related to patient's age

* State that he/she can see the specialty team

* If you are asked about time left for death answer "it is difficult to say"

* Explain that the relatives has no choice to decide particular treatment or intervention

* Explain that the treatment plan is a standard of care nationally and internationally and that the patient is unstable to be transferred anywhere

General:

* Offer calling a religious man

* Ask if the patient expressed any wishes for organ donation in the past or if the patient carry donation card

* State that she/he can see the patient, that the nurse will stay with her/him and that you will keep your contact number with the nurse for any further enquires or help

Chapter 7

Referral approach

SPKES Referral protocol

Setting:
* Review ED notes
* Introduce yourself
* Identify the receiving physician

Perception:

SBAR referral:

Situation:
* Core details: name, age, location and when came
* Why you are asked to see the patient?

Background:
Full history: presenting complaint, history of presenting complaint, past medical history, medications and allergies

Assessment:
Full observations, examination findings, investigations sent/received and pending and management so far

Recommendations:
Management plan

Knowledge:
* Put your statement: for example; I want you to come down to admit/see this patient
* Listen and summarize back

Empathy:
* Acknowledge anger
* Show empathy for busy shift for example
 *Offer glass of water, juice or coffee drink

Strategy:

Rational your statement

Avoid collusion

Agree appropriate plan: for example:
* Review the patient in ED
* Solve possible problems: arrange bed in ward with bed manager through the consultant
* Offer help in writing drug chart/admission notes, extract blood, arrange for investigations e.g. Echo, CT, and LP ... etc and starting emergency treatment e.g. giving first dose of antibiotic

Examples from previous exams

Cardiology referral

Case of chest pain with moderately high TIMI score
Rational your statement:
* TIMI score 3 or 4 carry 13 or 20% risk of death, new/recurrent MI or urgent revascularization at 14 days; so needs admission in CCU
* Components of TIMI score: age>65 years, known CAD/stenosis>50%, 3 risk factors of CAD (DM, HTN, hypercholesterolemia, smoking, family history of CAD), on aspirin in the last 7days, presented with 2 episodes of angina within last 24hours, abnormal ECG (ST deviation 0.5mm) and abnormal cardiac enzymes
* Not for discharge because of crescendo nature of pain (for example)
Avoid collusion:
* Don't agree repeating troponin I and discharge if negative
* Don't agree referral to RACPC (Rapid Assessment Chest Pain Clinic) with long waiting time
* Don't agree admission to normal ward, this patient should be admitted to CCU

Orthopedic referral

Case of Displaced distal radius fracture in an elderly patient after mechanical fall
Rational your statement:
* Displaced fracture needs ORIF (for example)
* Not for discharge because the patient is elderly, living alone and will require social worker assessment and fall clinic follow up (for example)
Avoid collusion:
* Don't agree applying back slab with clinic follow up

Neurosurgery referral

Case of VP shunt block or infection
Rational your statement:
* Patient with VP shunt who presented with features of increased ICP (confusion) and fever should be admitted to rule out shunt block or infection

Avoid collusion:

* Don't agree doing CBC and discharge if normal
* Don't agree giving antibiotic and observation in ED; you may agree doing LP, extracting basic bloods and blood culture and starting first dose of antibiotic, but only in case of accepting admission not observation in ED; so extracting blood and giving treatment in ED will not change the need for patient's assessment by the neurosurgeon and admission to rule out shunt block or infection

ITU referral

Case of severe pneumosepsis and DKA

Rationale your statement:

This patient needs ITU admission for invasive monitoring, possible inotropic support and mechanical ventilation

Avoid collusion:

Don't agree admission to the ward after stabilization in ED; the patient needs invasive monitoring

Agree appropriate plan:

What I would like to do next 2 hours while arranging a bed in ITU:

Sepsis six:

* Oxygen: to keep SPO2 94-98%; may need intubation (if shocked and not responded to the initial therapy or in case of impending respiratory failure)
* Blood culture: 2 sets are needed
* IV antibiotics: 1.2g co-amoxiclav and 500mg clarithromycin
* IV fluids: 1 liter boluses up to 60ml/kg or corrected hypovolaemia
* IFC: keep hourly UOP>0.5ml/kg
* Lactic acid

DKA management:

* Regular insulin IVI 0.1 unit/kg/hr
* Hourly glucose, blood gas and electrolytes check
* Add 10% dextrose to IV fluids if serum glucose<14mmol/L
* Add potassium to IV fluids as per protocol

What I recommend to be done in ITU:

EGDT-Resuscitation bundle:

* To keep CVP at least 8mmHg by giving IV fluids
* To keep MAP>65mmHg by giving nor epinephrine after achieving normovolaemia
* To keep Hct>30%, Hb 7-9g/dl and ScvO2>70% by giving blood and dobutamin infusion after achieving normovolaemia and adequate MAP

EGDT-Management bundle:

* Hydrocortisone 50mg IV every 6 hours
* To keep serum glucose 7-9mmol/L
* Permissive hypercapnoea: low TV (6ml/kg), high PEEP and to keep plateau pressure<30cmH2O

Chapter 8

Conflict resolution (CR) approach

SPKES CR protocol

Setting:
* Review ED notes
* Comfortable, confidential room without interruptions; close mobile and bleep
* Introduce yourself
* Identify patient or relative and his/her relation to the patient
* Consent from the patient to discuss his/her case

Perception:
* What do you know so far about the situation?
* Explain situation

Knowledge:
* Put your statement
* Listen and summarize back

Empathy:
* Acknowledge concern/anger and apologize
* Show empathy
* Offer glass of water, juice or coffee drink

Strategy:
Rational your statement
Avoid collusion
Agree appropriate plan

Examples from previous exams

Emergency contraception

Case of a mother who is angry for giving emergency contraception to her under age daughter without parents' consent

Put your statement:
Your daughter is young but she can give consent for treatment without parents' consent

Empathy:
* You can apologize by saying "I am sorry that you have these feelings towards us"
* You can show empathy by saying that teenagers at her age are difficult to treat

Rationale your statement:

* I will discuss with you the issues that worried you and what you already know unless getting permission from your daughter to discuss the details of this issue because your daughter still has the right for confidentiality

* I will discuss with you the process of decision making as documented in the ED notes:

1- First step: History taking: the doctor considered the possibility of pregnancy and STDs; you don't prefer that your daughter is getting pregnant or left with STDs untreated

2- Second step: Capacity assessment: the doctor assessed her capacity to give consent for treatment; capacity assessment → Gillick competence → children under age of 16 years can consent to medical treatment if they have sufficient maturity and judgment to enable them to fully understand what proposed → and your daughter was mature enough to realize that she needs help and to give the consent for treatment

3- Third step: Consent: the doctor discussed with her the benefits and risks of the treatment as well as the risks of not taking the treatment; risks of emergency contraceptive pills are nausea, vomiting, diarrhea and failure rate of 1%

Avoid collusion:

Don't break the patient's confidentiality to resolute the conflict

Agree appropriate plan:

Regarding daughter:

* Where is she now?

* If she is sick now ask if anybody can bring her to the hospital, If not tell the mother that you will ask the ambulance team to go to bring her.

* If she is ok now observe her, if she vomited during next couple of hours she should take another dose of the pills and if there is any abdominal pain during the next 2 months she should return back to ED

* She will be followed in the GP clinic for more discussion and education regarding methods of contraception, safe sex and for tracing the possibility of pregnancy and STDs.

Regarding mother:

* Open discussion with your daughter and try to be more close to her

* Group discussion with mothers who have daughters of same age group

* Official complaint if still unhappy

Bed manager

The bed manager wants to move unstable patient to avoid breach

Put your statement:

Keep the patient in the ED

Empathy:

You can acknowledge concern and show empathy by saying "I know that you are doing your work and that you want to achieve your targets"

Rationale your statement:

* Patient's observations still unstable
* Patient not seen by surgical team yet
* Discuss the significance of potential diagnosis of AAA (for example)
* Not in the best interest of the patient to be moved
 *Clinical breach is suitable in this case

Avoid collusion:

* Declines to speak individually with chief executive because that means that moving the patient is a possibility if a higher authority involved
* Don't agree to move sick patient to resolute the conflict

Agree appropriate plan:

* Review the patient yourself (if not done earlier)
* Call the surgical team to see the patient immediately
* Review other patients in the department to see if others are suitable to be moved
* Ask advice from duty consultant

NAI

Case of conflict with a nurse who disagree to admit a child to the pediatric ward as NAI because she knows the family

Put your statement:

I want to admit the patient to the pediatric ward as suspected case of NAI

Empathy:

* You can acknowledge concern and show empathy by saying "I can see that you know the parents and that makes more stress on you"
* There is always a possibility that the nurse is true, so don't lose the warm relationship with the hospital staff or parents and keep a return back way opened

Rationale your statement:

* Safety of the child is a priority
* It is in the best interest of the child to be investigated for NAI
* Story doesn't fit the injury or age of the child
* Other injuries are present
* Previous injuries are present
* The child is underweight, unkempt and smelly

Avoid collusion:

Don't agree to tell the family that the admission is not for NAI assessment

Agree appropriate plan:

* Admission for NAI workup
* Child will be assessed by a pediatrician and a social worker and they can confirm or refute the possibility of NAI

Chapter 9

Consent approach

The general approach

Introduction:
* Introduce yourself
* Identify the patient
* How old are you?
* What do you do for living?

Opening:
* Check patient's understanding of the situation: what do you know so far about your condition?
* Explain situation

Preparation:
* Patient's safety; Monitored area
* Patient's privacy; if appropriate
* Patient's comfort; offer pain killer
* Review the indication and contraindication from history, examination and investigation to establish that treatment or test is needed and or safe

Consent:
* Give information
* Explain benefits
* Discuss risks and how to avoid
* Offer alternatives

Plan:
Capacity assessment:
* Check patient's understanding and give time for reflection with the right to change his/her mind at any stage
* Check information retaining
* Check weighing risks and benefits
* Let the patient to communicate his/her decision clearly
Document capacity and the final decision

Examples from previous exams

Thrombolytic therapy

Consent for thrombolytic therapy in STEMI and PCI is not available
Review indication and contraindication:
History: AMPLE:
* Any Allergy to medicine?
* Any regular Medications? Blood thinner medication (warfarin) or clot/cotton busting medicine (previous streptokinase)
* Past medical and surgical history: haemophilia, severe liver disease, thrombocytopenia, stroke, recent surgery, trauma with or without resuscitation, proliferative eye bleeding, vitreous haemorrhage, upper/lower GI bleeding or serious vaginal bleeding
* Pregnancy
* Events: confirm events; for example confirm that events are suggestive of MI and ensure that there is no possibility of serious alternatives (aortic dissection – chest pain; shearing in nature and radiated to the back)
Examination:
* Look for high blood pressure; SBP>200mmgh and or DBP>120mmgh
* Look for unequal radial pulses or unequal blood pressure at both arms
Investigations:
* ECG: confirm STEMI
* CXR: look for aortic aneurysm/dissection
Consent:
Information:
We will give you a clot busting drug and there are two types; first one called streptokinase which is given as an infusion over one hour and is not given at all if you have allergy to it, if you received it before, if the infarct is big (anterior MI) or if your SBP is<90; the second drug named tenecteplase which is given as a single weight based dose through the vein as injection
Benefits:
30 early deaths are prevented per 1000 patients
Risks:
Bleeding risk<1%
Alternatives:
* Balloon (PCI): with risk of delay due to prolonged transfer but it is the best treatment if available immediately
* No treatment: with risk of death or risk to have poor heart function

Thromboprophylaxis

Consent for thromboprophylaxis in ambulatory trauma patient

Review indications and contraindications:

History: AMPLE:

As described earlier in thrombolytic therapy consent but add:

* Medications: combined oral contraceptive pills, hormone replacement therapy or tamoxifene

* Past medical and surgical history: cardiac failure, COPD, chronic renal failure or inflammatory bowel disease

* Major risk factors of PE: late pregnancy or post partum, previous VTE, major surgery, recent hospitalization or lower limb problems (fracture with cast or varicosities)

* Events: confirm events

Examination:

Look for high blood pressure; SBP>200mmgh and or DBP>120mmgh

Investigations:

Platelet count and eGFR

Consent:

Information:

You will be injected with a drug named clexane once daily subcutaneously until date of orthopaedic clinic review; the syringe is prefilled with the required dose (40 units), the dose will be adjusted to be lower (about 2/3 of the syringe dose) if there is renal impairment and you will be educated regarding injection technique or you will be referred to the district nurse for ongoing injections

Benefits:

The injection prevents clot (cotton) formation in your blood

Risks:

* Bleeding: if this happened stop the injections and seek medical advice

* Heparin Induced Thrombocytopenia (HIT): this is some sort of allergy to the injections which cause destruction of blood component named platelet and might cause bleeding and to be sure that everything is ok we will check your platelet count in 5 days if the clinic review is delayed and if it is low we will contact the haematologist for an alternative treatment

Alternatives:

* Oral pills/tablets: but its action is delayed as it takes about 3 days to start working

* No treatment: with a risk of developing clots in your blood and in this case we will contact a hematologist for advice

HIV test

Consent from patient for HIV test after needle stick injury of a staff nurse while extracting blood from that patient

Review indication (no contraindication):

Sex: review how to handle these sensitive questions from chapter 22:

* Hetero-bi-homosexual
* Unprotected sex
* Multiple partners
* Recent STDs and HIV status; do you or your partner have HIV and or STDs?

IVDU:

IVDU or shares needles: do you or your partner inject drugs or share needles?

Blood products and transfusions:

Do you or your partner has haemophilia or received any blood or blood products prior 1985 or received any blood transfusion in a developing country at any time?

Tattoo

Consent:

Information:

* First we will do a rapid finger prick test now; result will be available within one minute, then a three confirmatory blood tests are needed, we will extract blood now for the first test, the result will be available in few days in GU clinic (or GUM clinic) and further two tests will be needed after three and six months.
* Regarding confidentiality breaking; if the result is positive we have to find a way to inform your employer so he might be able to find another suitable job for you and I will discuss with my consultant the ideal way to do that.

Benefits:

* Benefit for the nurse: we will give Post Exposure Prophylaxis (PEP) for the injured nurse if the test is positive
* Benefit for you: HIV is treatable disease if diagnosed and treated early

Risks:

* Psychological upset if the test is positive
 *You may lose your job if the test is positive

Alternatives:

Don't perform the test or perform it later: in this situation we have to give PEP to our staff because you have high risk for HIV (for example)

Conscious sedation

Consent for conscious sedation from a patient who has a shoulder dislocation

Review indications and contraindications:

History: AMPLE:

Previous sedation or anesthesia with or without complications, medical co-morbidities and last meal

Examination:

* LEMON: Look, Evaluate 332, Mallampati, Obstruction and Neck mobility
* Chest
* Neurovascular examination of the limb

Investigations:

X ray (shoulder, chest) and ECG

Consent:

Information:

* We will perform movement to the shoulder while you are sedated; you will be sedated but you supposed to respond to conversations, you would breath normally without assistance and your blood pressure and all vital signs would be maintained without need for any support normally.
* You will be in a monitored area to monitor breathing, heart and blood pressure.
* Two doctors will be there, one to give sedation and the other to relocate the shoulder and one nurse will be there for assistance.

N.B: Details in the procedures chapter in part 2 of this book

Benefits:

Immediate safe relocation of the shoulder to the normal position with minimal pain

Risks:

* Risks of relocation: Failure, pain or injury (fracture or neurovascular); we will try to avoid these risks by applying minimal force
*Risks of sedation: hypotension or deep sedation (you may breath in your vomit); we will try to avoid these risks by giving minimal sedation, we will be in a well equipped and monitored area with well trained staff to deal with these risks and you might need support for breathing and blood pressure.

N.B: Details in the procedures chapter in part 2 of this book

Alternatives:

* Delayed relocation: but relocation will be difficult and risks will be higher
* Intra-articular lidocaine injection: but you will still feel pain
* General anesthesia: but with risks on lung, heart and blood pressure
* No treatment: you will lose the limb function, the shoulder will stiff in the new position and furthermore the abnormal position of the shoulder might press on nerves and vessels

Chapter 10

Counseling approach

The general approach

Introduction:
* Introduce yourself
* Identify the patient or the relative
* If you counsel a relative of a child/patient: What is the child's/patient's name? How old is she/he? What is your relation to her/him? Any parental responsibility?

Opening:
* Check the patient's/relatives' understanding of the situation: what do you know so far about your/her/his condition?
* Explain situation

Brief history

Counselling:
* Definition
* Causes
* Diagnosis
* Treatment
* Prognosis

Plan:
* Idea-Concern-Expectation (ICE): Idea (what do you think or what is your thoughts regarding this problem?), Concern (what do you worry about?) and Expectation (what do you expect from us to do?)
* Offer leaflets instructions
* Follow up for example with asthma nurse or diabetes nurse
* If the patient for discharge tell the relative/patient the return back instructions

Examples from previous exams

N.B: Source of information: patient.co.uk

Gastroenteritis

Counsel mother of a child with gastroenteritis
History:
Warning flags in the history:
1- Age<1 year or low birth weight
2- Vomiting blood, unable to keep anything down or if it persists>2 days

3- Diarrhea if bloody, worsening or not settled>4 days

4- Tummy pain which is severe

5- Temperature especially if high grade

6- Dehydration: dry lips/tongue, no tears while crying, dry nappies, lack of energy, drowsy, pale/mottled skin or cold hands/feet

7- Feeding: if stopped or doesn't drink much

8- Co morbidities: diabetes, cardiac disease or recent hospitalization

9- Medications: Antibiotics, steroids or chemotherapy

10- Travel: if you suspect catching infection abroad

Counseling:

Definition:

Infection of gut

Causes:

* Most commonly virus (rota virus or adenovirus)

* May be bacteria (food poisoning) or other germs

Diagnosis:

By typical symptoms and investigations are rarely needed

Treatment:

* Usually self limited illness and settled within few days

* The aim of treatment is to prevent lack of body fluids (dehydration) by encouraging the child to take plenty of fluids as well as to continue normal diet, usual drinks and breast/bottle feeding but to avoid fruit juices or fizzy drinks

* Rehydration drinks are useful if your child is at high risk of dehydration or have mild dehydration → it provides perfect balance of water, salts and sugar → the small amounts of salt and sugar helps water to be absorbed better from gut into the body

* Anti-secretory medicines can reduce the amount of water that released into gut and can be given to the children>3 months old

* If the child vomit; wait 5 minutes and try giving fluids again more slowly

* The amount of fluids you give depend on your child age, weight and amount and frequency of vomiting and diarrhoea

* As a rule; rehydrate before giving solids

* Sometimes the child may need admission to be treated with fluids given through a tube passes through child's nose to stomach or giving fluids directly to vein; that is in case of severe dehydration or if the child unable to keep fluids down but at the other hand the unnecessary use of IV fluids could cause acidosis beside putting a line in a child is difficult and painful

* Paracetamol and Ibuprofen can be given for fever and pain

* How to prevent spread? Hand washing, clean objects and surfaces and breast feeding

* Immunization: oral drops at 2 and 3 months for rota virus

* Antibiotics/stool microscopy and culture: if there is bloody diarrhoea, high fever, if catch infection abroad, if the child had recent hospitalization or recent treatment with antibiotics

Asthma

Counsel mother of a child with asthma

History:

* Symptoms severity: cough, wheeze, breathlessness or chest tightness
* Atopy: hay fever or eczema
* Family history of asthma: because it runs in some families

Counseling:

Definition:

It is a condition that affects the smaller airways/tubes (bronchioles) of the lungs and from time to time the airways narrow in people who have asthma.

Causes:

* It caused by inflammation of the airways and it is not known why the inflammation occurs. The inflammation irritates the muscles around the airways and causes them to squeeze, this causes narrowing of the airways, it is then more difficult for air to get in and out of the lungs and this causes wheezes and breathlessness. The inflammation also causes the lining of the airways to make extra mucus which causes cough and further obstruction of the airways.
* Asthma symptoms may flare up from time to time and there is often no obvious reason why symptoms flare up; however some people find that symptoms are triggered or made worse in certain situations → infections (cold), pollens, moulds, exercise, medicine (ibuprofen), smoking and cigarette fumes

Diagnosis:

Peak Flow Meter (PFM) is a small device that patient blows into; it measures the speed of air that patient can blow out of his/her lung, the readings will be low if his/her airways are narrowed if patient have untreated asthma and the readings will improve when the airways are opened up with treatment so regular readings can be used to help assess how well treatment is working.

Treatment:

* Reliever inhaler: taken as required to relieve symptoms as it relaxes the muscles in the airways
* Preventer inhaler: taken every day to prevent symptoms from developing and it contains steroids; it works by reducing inflammation in the airways, its onset is delayed, duration is prolonged and taken whether there is symptoms or no but bone strength may be reduced following steroid use so be sure to have good supply of calcium in diet (milk and bread)
* Learn how to use inhalers correctly
* Explain the spacer devices with and without mask if appropriate
* See doctor if symptoms not fully controlled
* See doctor urgently if symptoms are severe
* Influenza immunization every autumn

* Asthma action plan: a plan agreed between patient and his/her doctor enable patient to make adjustments to the dose of inhalers depending on symptoms and PFM readings

Prognosis:
* Half of the children who develop asthma grow out of it by the time they are adults
* Although not curable it is treatable and stepping up treatment for a while during bad spells will often control symptoms

Chicken pox

Counsel a pregnant lady who is concerned about contact with her chicken pox child

History:
For the child, pregnant lady and other family members:
1- Current chicken pox symptoms: what? When started?
2- Past history of chicken pox
3- Warning flags: Chronic lung disease, smoking, on steroids or on chemotherapy
4- Pregnancy history: how many weeks pregnant?

Counseling:
Definition:
Infection affecting respiratory tract and skin
Causes:
Varicella Zoster Virus (VZV); it is infectious from 2 days before the spots first appear until they have all crusted over (usually 5 days after the spots appear) and it spreads by face to face contact such in conversation or if you are in the same room with the patient for>15 minutes

Diagnosis and prevention:
* Diagnosis by typical manifestations: URTI symptoms and rash
* When you have chicken pox your immune system makes protein called antibodies; these fight the virus and then provide lifelong protection against it (immunity) and most of people have this immunity, however if you missed it as a child and get it as an adult it is usually more severe and complications are more common particularly if you are pregnant
* If you are not sure that if you are immune or no do blood test; if antibodies present you are immune and no further action needed but if you are not immune you have to take an injection called immunoglobulin which contains antibodies to the chicken pox virus and it is best taken within 4 days of contact with the virus but it could be given up to 10 days
* Antibodies and immunoglobulin pass placenta to protect the baby

Treatment:
* Treatment of the mother: If you have chicken pox rash you will be treated with acyclovir which should be started within 24 hours of rash first appearing then daily review in the hospital putting in mind to come immediately to the hospital if there is chest symptoms, neurological symptoms, hemorrhagic or dense rash or bleeding; if you have any of these warning symptoms or if you have any one of the warning flags as described earlier you will need admission to the hospital for intensive treatment.
* Treatment of the child: it is a self limiting mild disease in children unless the child has one of the warning flags described earlier in the history; treatment is almost symptomatic and contains calamine lotion, paracetamol and might be antibiotics for secondary bacterial infection.
* Isolation is needed for chicken pox patients
Complications:
* Complications to the mother: inflammation of lungs, brain, heart muscles and kidneys
* Complications to the unborn baby: Fetal Varicella Syndrome (FVS) → congenital anomalies

Chapter 11

Pediatric history taking approach

The general approach

Introduction:
* Introduce yourself
* Identify the adult and ask "what is your relation to the child? Do you have parental responsibility?"
* How old are you? What do you do for living?
* Where is the child? What is his/her name? How old is he/she?

Presenting complaint:
* What's brought you in today? Can you tell me more about that? Or ask simply how can I help you?
* Listen as long as appropriate
* Offer pain killers if appropriate
* Check patient's stability and that patient doesn't need immediate treatment

History of presenting complain:
Nature and characters of the complaint:
You have to ask about:
* ODPARA as described in chapter 1
* SOCRATES: mainly for pain assessment:
Site – Where is the pain? Or the maximal site of the pain.
Onset – When did the pain start, and was it sudden or gradual? Include also whether if it is progressive or regressive.
Character – What is the pain like? An ache? Stabbing?
Radiation – Does the pain radiate anywhere?
Associations – Any other symptoms associated with the pain?
Time course – Does the pain follow any pattern?
Exacerbating/Relieving factors – Does anything change the pain? Or Anything make it worse or better?
Severity – How bad is the pain? (On scale from 0 to 10 when 0 is no pain and 10 is the maximum pain)

General points:
* Any previous similar episodes or ED attendances?
* Any other family members affected?
* Any contact with sick patient?
* Any notification from nursery or school of prevalent illness?
* Any medicines tried at home? Did it work?
* Any trauma?
* Any temperature?
* Any recent illness? URTI or diarrhoea

Infants:
* Feeds: How is his/her feed? Is it ok? Ask about intervals (how often?), quantity (how much?) and breast/bottle or both (Do you breast feed or bottle feed him/her or both?)
* Vomits: Any nausea (feeling sick), Any vomiting (being sick)? Ask about frequency (How often?), timing with feed (Dose it follow certain pattern?), quantity (How much?) and nature (Projectile)
* Bowels: Any change in bowel motion? Any diarrhoea or constipation? And any blood or mucus in stool?
* Wet nappies: how often does he/she wet his/her nappies?
* Sleep pattern: Any change in sleep pattern?
* Crying: Any excessive crying? Is it consolable or not?
* Weight: Any change in weight? Gain/loss? Have you plotted it on the growth chart?

Past medical, surgical history and hospitalization:
* Any acute or chronic medical problems?
* Any previous surgery?
* Any previous hospitalization?

MAFTOS (Medications, Allergies, Family history, Travel history, Social history):
Medications and allergies:
* Any doctor prescribed drugs? What is the name of these drugs? What is the dosages? How he/she took it? Oral? Injection? How frequent?
* Any over the counter drugs/homeopathic drugs?
* Any allergy to medicine?
Family history:
* Any illnesses running in the family?
* Any illnesses suffered by parents and siblings?
Social history:
* Living circumstances: Where is he/she live?
* Family members at home and in contact with the child: Who lives with him/her? You may need to ask about the relationship of the child with the new partner if you are suspecting abuse from step father/mother
* Social service input → past and present
* Domestic violence
* Nursery or school attending → happy there? Educational progress? Bullying problems? Impact of illness on it?
* Any smoking, alcohol drink or drug use?

BIRD (Birth history, Immunization, Red book, Development history):
Birth history:
* Any mother issue during pregnancy? (Infections, Rh incompatibility or recreational drug use)
* Any child issue during pregnancy, delivery or after delivery? (Type of delivery, any support required as CPAP or NICU and any concern regarding baby check or weight after delivery?)
Immunization:
* Schedule adhered to?
* Reason for missed immunization?

Development history:
Are milestones being achieved? Or simply ask how is his/her development? Or how is he/she growing? Is it normal? (Sitting, crawling, walking, talking, toilet training and nocturnal continence)

Closing:
* Idea-Concern-Expectation (ICE): Idea (what do you think or what is your thoughts regarding this problem?), Concern (what do you worried about?) and Expectation (what do you expect from us to do?)
* Anything else you feel I should know?
* Explain DD and likely diagnosis
* Explain what you will do next (examination, investigations or consultation)
* Any questions?
* Thank you

Examples from previous exams

Non Accidental Injury (NAI)

Opening instead of presenting complaint:
* Check parent's understanding of the situation: what do you know so far about the situation?
* Explain situation

History of presenting complaint:
* Ask about timing, mechanism and circumstances of the injury
* Any previous injuries for the same child or other sibling?
* Any previous hospital/health care contact for the same child or other sibling?
* Ask about the reason behind the delayed presentation?
* Any recent change in the behaviour of the child?

Plan:
* Local examination: I will examine the injury and the limb
* General examination: I will undress the child to do general examination and to look for other injuries
* Manage current injury: pain killer, arm sling, splint, x ray, cast, wound management and referral to orthopaedic doctor or surgeon
* Paediatric doctor referral: I will call the paediatric team to review the child for suspected NAI and to admit him for further workup
* Social services referral: I will involve social services to investigate this case and I need to protect other siblings with immediate effect so I will send an emergency social worker round to check them
* Rule of security/police: you will not be allowed to take the child home and I will call security/police if you try to leave but I can't physically restrain you or remove the child from you unless police involved

* Legal issues: say "the case could be NAI or not but anyhow you may be blamed at least for delayed presentation"

Limping child

DD:

All ages	Toddlers (age 1-3)	Age 4-10	Adolescents (age 11-16)
* Septic arthritis * Osteomyelitis * Trauma (fractures, soft tissue injuries, foreign bodies) * Neoplasm * Sickle cell crisis * Cellulitis * Haemarthrosis * Regional lymphadenitis * Henoch-Schonlein purpura * Non accidental injury	* Developmental dysplasia of the hip * Toddlers fractures * Transient synovitis * Neuromuscular: cerebral palsy, muscular dystrophy	* Transient synovitis * Perthes' disease * Kohler's disease	* Slipped upper femoral epiphysis

Plan:
* Examination
* Investigation: blood tests, probably joint aspiration if there is fever or suspicion of septic arthritis or US hip if there is hip pain
* Treatment and disposition depend on the diagnosis: review the topic from any text book
* If you considered NAI follow the same plan of NAI as described earlier

Dental abscess

History of presenting complaint:
* Eye symptoms: red eye, discharge, loss of vision and painful or weak eye movement
* Sinus symptoms: nasal discharge or headache
* Complications (Meningitis and septicemia): unwell, lack of energy (lethargy), neck pain and rash

Plan:

I am concerned about infection in teeth that might be spreaded to the eye (Dental abscess caused Orbital cellulitis) so what we will do now is:

* Vital signs and examination
* Blood tests including blood culture
* Admission in pediatric ward for IV antibiotics
* Ophthalmology and dental doctor opinion
* Imaging might be requested to confirm eye infection
* Operation might be needed if there is eye infection not responded to antibiotic treatment
* If you considered neglect or NAI follow the same plan of NAI as described earlier

Child who ingested ecstasy

History of presenting complaint:

You can apply ODPARA as described before putting in your mind the following:

* Any recent change in his/her behavior? If yes, what kind of changes you noticed in his/her behavior? And since when? For how long he/she behaving like this? How frequent? Any relation to specific time of the day (does it follow any pattern?)?
* Any seizures? Loss of consciousness? Limb numbness or weakness?

DD:

Infection (systemic or neurological), Brain tumor, Head trauma, electrolytes disturbances or Drug ingestion

Plan:

I am concerned that he might ingest drugs and what we will do now:

* Vital signs and examination
* Blood tests
* Admission in paediatric ward for further work up and observation
* If you considered neglect in this case follow the same plan as described in NAI

UTI

History of presenting complaint:

* Upper UTI symptoms: loin pain, vomiting and fever
* Lower UTI symptoms: dysuria, haematuria, frequency and offensive smelling urine

Past history:

Congenital urinary tract disease or previous intervention (contrast/dye test or surgery)

Family history:

VU reflux or renal disease

Plan:
* Vital signs and examination
* Blood tests if indicated → in suspected upper UTI
* Urine test: <3 years old → lab test (microscopy), >3 years old → bedside test (urine dipstick)
* Most of cases are managed with oral antibiotic (duration depend on site and presence of complications) and GP review within 48 hours → if no response → KUB Ultrasound
* Few cases will need admission for IV antibiotics: if septic, unwell child or if he is vomiting and can't take the oral medicines

Purpuric rash

History of presenting complaint:
* Rash: initial site, color, palpable or not and blanchable or not
* Neurological symptoms: neck pain, limb numbness/weakness, seizure or confusion
* Leukemia: Anemia symptoms → tired, SOB on exertion or palpitation; Thrombocytopenia symptoms → easy bruising with minimal trauma; Leucopenia → recurrent infections
* HSP: joint pain, tummy pain or hematuria
DD:
Meningococcal disease, HSP, Thrombocytopenia (ITP, leukemia, aplastic anemia or septic shock), viral illness and trauma/NAI
Plan:
* Vital signs (hypertension in HSP) and examination (skin, liver, spleen, lymph nodes, neurological and meningism)
* Blood test: low platelets → ITP and renal failure → HSP
* Urine tests: haematuria in HSP
* Disposition depends on the diagnosis; for example in HSP discharge the child home with clinic follow up unless complicated (hypertension or renal impairment)

Chapter 12

Chest pain history taking approach

Introduction:
* Wash your hands
* Introduce yourself
* Identify the patient
* Consent for chatting
* How old are you?
* What do you do for living?

Presenting complaint:
* As described earlier in chapter 11
* Mention that you will put the patient on monitor and that you will perform ECG
* It is unlikely to deal with a patient needs immediate treatment in a history taking station but you have to be aware of it

History of presenting complaint:
* ODPARA: as described earlier in chapter 1
* SOCRATES: as described earlier in chapter 11, it is unlikely to face the diagnosis of Aortic Dissection (AD) in a history taking station but it is important to show that it is in your mind by asking if the chest pain is sudden in onset and shearing in character that radiates to the back
* Any palpitation/heart racing? Any shortness of breath?
* Any nausea (feeling sick), vomiting (being sick) or sweating?
* Any cough, Sputum (phlegm), Blood in phlegm or temperature (fever)?
* Any trauma?
* Any dysphagia (difficult swallowing), indigestion or epigastric pain (tummy pain)?
* Any limb pain or swelling?
* Any previous similar episodes?

Past medical, surgical history and hospitalization:
* Any previous heart attack?
* Any chronic illnesses like heart vessels disease (Coronary Artery Disease), diabetes, hypertension or hypercholesterolemia (IHD risk factors)
* Any previous heart surgery like balloon (angiography)?
* Any other heart problems like rheumatic fever
* Any previous clot in limb or lung? Any recent surgery, limb problem/fracture, recent reduced mobility, tumours (growth) or pregnancy? (PE major risk factors)
* Any previous stroke, Transient Ischemic Attack or Peripheral Vascular Disease (Vascular diseases)
* Any previous peneumothorax (air around or outside the lungs)?

MAFTOS (Medications, Allergies, Family history, Travel history, Social history):

Medications and allergies:
* Oral Contraceptive Pills (OCP) are a risk of PE
* Cardiac medicines: Aspirin, nitrates (sublingual pills that relieves chest pain) or beta blocker (pills that control heart beats/racing)
* Anticoagulants (blood thinners): heparin injections or warfarin pills (ask about last INR result)
* Any previous contrast/dye test? Any allergy to it?
* Any treatment for diabetes? Metformin should stopped for a couple of days if contrast/dye test needed
* Any treatment to control blood pressure
* Any allergy to medicine?

Family history:
Any illnesses run in the family or suffered by parents like hypertension, Ischemic Heart Disease (IHD), MI (heart attack), congenital heart disease or spontaneous pneumothorax?

Social history:
* Smoking: do you smoke? If yes ask about the details (pack years), if he is not currently smoking ask him if he is ex smoker? Then ask about details and if he never smokes in the present or in the past ask him about passive smoking.
* Alcohol: any alcohol drinks?
* Recreational drugs: any drug use? Cocaine (crack – smoked, coke – snorted, eaten or injected) and marijuana can cause heart attack
* Any impact on Activities of Daily Living (ADLs), work or hobbies?

Closing:
As described in chapter 11 earlier

DD:
MI, PE, AD, spontaneous pneumothorax, pneumonia with or without pleural effusion or musculoskeletal

Plan:
* Manage the patient in monitored area and request ECG and vital signs; again remember to measure blood pressure in both arms to look for AD and give oxygen if indicated.
* Examination of cardiovascular and respiratory system
* Perform CXR to look for cardiomegaly, pneumothorax or AD
* Perform blood tests like troponin I or D-dimer (no major risk factor for PE and alternative diagnosis is more likely than PE)
* Treatment and disposition depends on the diagnosis:
Some indications of admission:
1- Cocaine related chest pain as it causes vasospasm and could be fatal
2- Angina with TIMI score 3 or above but stable angina with TIMI score 1 or 2 can be discharged with clinic follow up
3- Acute Coronary Syndrome (unstable angina, NSTEMI or STEMI – balloon or thrombolytic therapy)
4- PE: heparin, CTPA (major risk factor for PE &or PE is more likely than alternative diagnosis) and venous Doppler US (scan of the limb vessels)

Chapter 13

Shortness of breath history taking approach

The general approach

Introduction:
* As described in chapter 12 earlier
* Job and exposures are very important: ask about current as well as previous job and ask about exposure to asbestos, animals or birds
Presenting complaint:
* As described earlier in chapter 12
* Offer to listen to chest if extremely shortness of breath and administer oxygen or nebulizer if required
History of presenting complaint:
* ODPARA: as described earlier in chapter 1
* Severity: ask about exercise tolerance, orthopnoea and Paroxysmal Nocturnal Dyspnoea (PND)
* Any chest pain?
* Any palpitation (heart racing)?
* Any fatigue (feeling tired) or lack of energy (lethargy)? (anaemia symptoms)
* Any cough, Sputum (phlegm), Blood in phlegm, temperature (fever) or night sweating?
* Any wheeze (noisy breathing)?
* Any URTI symptoms?
* Any contact with ill patient? (influenza or TB)
* Any loss of weight, loss of appetite or lumps anywhere in your body? (symptoms of growth)
* Any sudden onset of flushing, itching, rash, facial/lips/tongue swelling or voice change/hoarseness of voice (symptoms of allergic reaction)
* Any trauma?
* Any reduction of urine amount or change in its color?
* Clues for primary hyperventilation: dizziness, circumoral parasthesia, carpopedal spasm, previous similar episodes or previous panic attacks?
N.B: primary hyperventilation is a diagnosis of exclusion
Past medical, surgical history and hospitalization:
As described earlier in chapter 12 but add:
* Any previous asthma or tubes narrowing (COPD)?
* Any previous TB, lung infection or seasonal influenza?
* Any previous eczema or hay fever (atopy)?
* Any previous kidney disease?

MAFTOS (Medications, Allergies, Family history, Travel history, Social history):

Medications and allergies:

As described earlier in chapter 12 but beware that:

* NSAIDs might exacerbates asthma

* Ask about treatment with home oxygen, home nebulizers and inhalers

* Ask about use of water tablets

* Ask about use of a tocolytic (medicine to delay delivery) if the patient is pregnant as some of these medicines might cause palpitation, SOB or chest pain

* Ask about use of Epo injections (Erythropoietin) in case of kidney failure

Family history:

As described earlier in chapter 12 but add family history of atopy (asthma) or TB

Social history:

* As described earlier in chapter 12 but be aware that crack cocaine can cause airway burns

* Life style: stress and anxiety might cause primary hyperventilation

Closing:

As described earlier in chapter 11

DD:

Primary hyperventilation

Secondary hyperventilation:

* Cardiac: MI, arrhythmia or cardiogenic pulmonary oedema

* Respiratory: PE, asthma, COPD, pneumothorax, pneumonia or pleural effusion

* Renal: fluid overload or uraemia and metabolic acidosis

* Metabolic acidosis: DKA, sepsis, heart failure or uraemia

* Pain, trauma, hypoxia or hypovolaemia

* Poisoning: aspirin, methanol, carbon monoxide, cyanide or ethylene glycol

Plan:

As described earlier in chapter 12 but be aware that:

* Give nebulizer if required if not already given

* AD is not presented with SOB alone

* Measure Peak Expiratory Flow Rate (PEFR) or Peak Flow Meter (PFM) as a part of respiratory examination

* It is not uncommon for pregnant women to present with SOB so do CXR if indicated and use abdominal shield to protect the foetus

* Blood tests: in addition to troponin I and D dimer do CBC/chemistry/blood gas and BNP to look for causes of secondary hyperventilation

Examples from previous exams

Renal dialysis

Renal history:
Dialysis:
* Why you are on dialysis?
* When did it first start?
* Where? Are you known to the hospital renal team?
* What pattern of dialysis you are on? Venous? Peritoneal?
* How frequent?
* When was the last session? Any problems happened during the last session?
* When will you go for the next session?
Fluid balance:
* Do you produce normal urine amount and color?
* Any recent reduction in urine amount or change in urine color?
* What is your normal dry weight? I mean the weight after dialysis session?
* Any recent weight gain?
* How much do you drink and eat every day?
* Any recent increase in the amount of daily drinks and foods?
* Any poor compliance with fluid restriction?
* Explain this simple equation: more fluids + low urine = fluid overload
Uraemia:
* Any restless legs, cramps or bone ache?
* Any loss of appetite, feeling sick or being sick?
* Any itching?
* Any general weakness, fatigue or confusion?
Plan:
* Identify and start management steps for: hyperkalemia, metabolic acidosis, uremic encephalopathy or fluid overload
* Contact his/her normal renal team to continue emergency management or for arrangement of urgent management

Breathlessness in pregnant lady

Pregnancy history:
* Gravida? Para? Miscarriages? How many weeks pregnant?
* Any previous follow up, blood tests or scans during this pregnancy?
* Any problem in this or any previous pregnancy?
* Any previous similar episodes in this or previous pregnancy?

DD:

Gradual breathlessness during first and second trimesters:
* Physiological breathlessness
* Anaemia

Acute or sudden breathlessness:
* Respiratory: PE or pneumothorax
* Cardiac: pericardial tamponade, angina, AD or arrhythmias
* Anaphylaxis

Breathlessness associated with acute cough:
* URTI or LRTI
* Exacerbation of chronic lung disease (asthma or COPD)

Breathlessness associated with noisy breathing (wheezes):
* Bronchial asthma
* Cardiac asthma

Near term breathlessness with pulmonary and peripheral edema:
* Sever pre-eclampsia/eclampsis
* Tocolytic induced pulmonary oedema
* Cardiogenic pulmonary oedema (pre-existing cardiac disease or peripartum cardiomyopathy)
* Amniotic fluid embolism

Plan:
* Depends on the diagnosis
* If you suspected PE then perform V/Q scan which has low risk to fetus
* Perform at least bedside fetus scan for all patients but you might need even to request CTG or involve obstetric team

Exercise induced asthma

Plan:
You will probably found normal examination and investigations and your disposition might be:
* Reassurance and short counselling: as described in chapter 10
* GP follow up for further tests and to prescribe regular& or before exercise inhalers

COPD

Plan:
Explain the plan to the patient in appropriate words:
* Controlled oxygen therapy, air driven nebulizers and explain why
* Blood gas and Non Invasive Ventilation (NIV)
* Blood & or sputum cultures and antibiotics
* Steroids

Chapter 14

Leg swelling history taking approach

Introduction:
As described earlier in chapter 12
Presenting complaint:
As described earlier in chapter 13
History of presenting complaint:
* ODPARA: as described earlier in chapter 1
* One or both legs?
* Any swelling elsewhere? (Tummy – ascitis, back, genital – scrotal/labial, facial – periorbital/lips/tongue and arms)
* Any pain? If yes where (legs, tummy or chest)?
* Any previous similar episodes?
* Any reduced mobility? (Reduced mobility is a common benign physical cause of bilateral leg swelling but if it is associated with unilateral leg swelling you have to rule out DVT)
* Renal history as described earlier in chapter 13
* Symptoms suggesting Post Streptococcal Glomerulonephritis (PSGN): haematuria and oliguria preceded by either URTI or skin infection
* Symptoms suggestive of Systemic Lupus Erythematosis (SLE) and Lupus Nephritis (LN): oliguria preceded by history of rash, joints pain and mouth ulcers (sores)
* Symptoms suggestive of Hemolytic Uremic Syndrome (HUS): oilguria preceded by fever, vomiting and bloody diarrhea
* Symptoms of heart failure: dyspnoea, orthopnoea or PND
* Symptoms of liver failure: Any yellow discoloration of skin or eye white? Any bruising? Any history of vomiting blood?
* Symptoms of protein losing enteropathy: Any change in bowel habits (loose motion)?
* Symptoms of anemia: easy fatigability, tired, SOB on mild exertion or heart racing? (Anemia itself might cause generalized body swelling or it might be associated with any chronic illness or renal failure)
* Symptoms of hypothyroidism: Any cold intolerance, voice tone change or low concentration?
Past medical, surgical history and hospitalization:
* Any previous diabetes (? Diabetic nephropathy or nephrotic syndrome) or hypertension (? Secondary hypertension due to long standing renal disease)?
* Any previous kidney, heart, liver, bowel or thyroid disease?
* Any previous lupus disease?

MAFTOS (Medications, Allergies, Family history, Travel history, Social history):

Medications and allergies:

* Ay regular medicine for high blood pressure (CCB and captopril) or diabetes (insulin or oral hypoglycaemic)?

* Any medicines for heart or water tablets?

* Any regular use of NSAIDs? (it might cause renal disease)

* Any allergy to medicine?

Family history:

Any illnesses running in the family or suffered by parents like kidney diseases (polycystic kidney disease or reflux nephropathy), lupus disease or hereditary angioneurotic oedema?

Social history:

As described earlier in chapter 12 but beware that:

* Injecting drugs might give a clue to the diagnosis of liver disease

* Diet: malnutrition and salty diets might cause generalized body swelling

* Sexual history: might needed if hepatitis and chronic liver disease are suspected

Closing:

As described earlier in chapter 12

DD:

* Renal failure and fluid overload

* Congestive Heart Failure (CHF)

* Hypoproteinaemia: liver failure, nephrotic syndrome, protein losing entropathy and malnutrition

* Anemia

* Hypothyroidism

* Medications (CCB for example)

* Hereditary angioneurotic edema

Plan:

If you suspect pulmonary edema follow the same plan as described earlier in chapter 13 otherwise explain the following key steps to either examiner or patient as requested in the question:

* *Vital signs:*

Blood pressure and random blood sugar

* *Urine dipstick and analysis:*

Look for:

1- Proteinuria: if positive it means that there is a kidney disease and next step will to quantify proteinuria by measurement of spot urine protein: creatinin ratio → significant proteinuria present if the ratio is >15mg/mmol and Nephrotic range proteinuria start from ratio >350mg/mmol. Causes of proteinuria either primary (glomerulonephritis or tubular disease) or secondary (diabetes, hypertension, SLE, CHF or vasculitis)

2- Haematuria and RBCs casts

Examination:
General (anemia, malnutrition), cardiovascular, respiratory, abdominal, back and limbs

ECG:
Hyperkalemic changes (renal failure) or low voltage ECG (heart failure)

CXR:
Pulmonary edema due to either heart failure or renal failure

Blood tests:
CBC, chemistry, electrolytes, renal profile, liver profile including INR, BNP, albumin and cholesterol (nephrotic syndrome → hypercholesterolemia)

Disposition depends on the most likely diagnosis:
Let's take nephrotic syndrome as an example:
-- Indications of kidney team referral:
1- Significant proteinuria with spot urine protein : creatinine ration>100mg/mmol
2- Mild proteinuria with spot urine protein : creatinine ration>50mg/mmol with presence of other features of kidney disease (hypertension, hematuria and renal impairment)
3- Any proteinuria with presence of other features of kidney disease and features of systemic disease as well (? SLE)
-- Kidney team will do:
1 - Aggressive blood pressure control: use ACEIs or ARBs
2 - Further tests and follow up (kidney scan, immunology screen – SLE, serology screen – hepatitis that might cause nephrotic syndrome and finally kidney biopsy for the final diagnosis)

Chapter 15

Palpitation history taking approach

Introduction:
As described earlier in chapter 12

Presenting complaint:
* As described earlier in chapter 12
* Any palpitation now?
* Be aware of the adverse effects of arrhythmias and screen it quickly: Any hypotension, chest pain, SOB, syncope or lightheaded now

History of presenting complaint:
* ODPARA: as described earlier in chapter 1
* Frequency: how frequent?
* Nature: is it regular or irregular and is it fast or slow?
* Symptoms suggestive of hypoglycemia: sweating, nausea, vomiting and dizziness
* Any syncope? Ask about suggestive criteria of cardiac syncope: exertional syncope or syncope in supine position
* Symptoms suggestive of IHD: chest pain or SOB
* Symptoms suggestive of PE (chest pain or SOB), asthma (SOB or noisy breathing) or hypoxia (agitation or confusion)
* Symptoms suggestive of hyperthyroidism: tired, nervous, weak, weight loss, heat intolerance, sweating, tremor/shaking, vision disturbances, eye pain, swelling in throat/neck, swallowing difficulty, diarrhea or menstrual cycles abnormalities (light menses)
* Are you pregnant?
* Symptoms suggestive of anemia or bleeding
* Symptoms suggestive of dehydration (lack of body fluids): vomiting, diarrhea, low urine amount, dry lips and mouth
* Symptoms suggestive of infection: for example ask any temperature (fever)? Then do systemic review
* Any previous similar episodes?

Past medical, surgical history and hospitalization:
* AF risk factors: hypertension, thyroid disease, heart disease (valvular – history of rheumatic fever or IHD)
* IHD and PE risk factors: as described earlier in chapter 12
* Previous structural heart disease (cardiomyopathy for example)

MAFTOS (Medications, Allergies, Family history, Travel history, Social history):
Medications and allergies:
As described earlier in chapter 12 and add thyroxin, beta blockers withdrawal or beta 2 agonist inhalers
Family history:
As described earlier in chapter 12 but add family history of sudden death

Social history:

As described earlier in chapter 12 and be aware of:

* Alcohol excess or withdrawal might cause arrhythmias especially AF

* It is not uncommon to see in the exam coffee, tea or chocolate induced palpitation so diet history is very important

* Life style: stress and anxiety

Closing:

As described earlier in chapter 12

DD:

* Hypoglycaemia

* IHD → arrhythmias due to low cardiac muscles perfusion

* PE or asthma → tachyarrhythmia due to hypoxia

* Thyroid disease (hyperthyroidism)

* Pregnancy

* Anaemia

* Infections and fever

* Dehydration and electrolytes imbalance

* Medications, illicit drugs, alcohol excess or withdrawal, caffeine and stress/anxiety

Plan:

As described earlier in chapter 13, read the following key steps for more awareness:

* *Monitored area and attach to monitor*

* *Vital signs including random blood sugar and SPO2*

* *Examination:*

Cardiovascular, respiratory, thyroid state (including GI, neurological and cognitive function examinations)

* *ECG if not already done:*

- Twelve lead ECG recording is clearly the primary diagnostic test and if temporally correlated with symptoms of palpitations this will have a very high yield revealing the presence or absence of an underlying arrhythmia; if this is the case, a confident diagnosis can be made.

- In the absence of the patient actually having palpitations at the time that the ECG is recorded, the trace must be examined closely for the following:

1- Pre-excitation e.g. Wolf Parkinson White Syndrome

2- P Wave abnormalities

3- Left ventricular hypertrophy

4- Abnormal QRST morphology e.g. Brugada syndrome

5- Frequent ventricular premature beats

6- Q waves

7- Abnormal QT duration (long and short)

8- Atrioventricular block

9- Fascicular block

Any of these abnormalities may indicate a potential underlying aetiology for the presenting symptoms: Pre-excitation may indicate recurrent SVT, prolonged QT interval and findings suggestive of Brugada Syndrome may herald recurrent VT, atrioventricular block may produce symptomatic bradyarrhythmias, etc.

* CXR:

Look for chest infection as a cause of fever if it is the case or look for cardiomegaly

* Urine dipstick:

Look for urine infection

* Blood tests:

Troponin I, D-dimer, blood gas, CBC, chemistry, electrolytes, thyroid function test, pregnancy test (Bhcg) and cultures

* Management in the Emergency Department

- Is intervention required?

The patient may be displaying an arrhythmia on ECG monitoring at the time of assessment. If this is the case manage the arrhythmia as per current guidelines and identify & treat the underlying cause

- Admission criteria in asymptomatic patients without demonstrable arrhythmia for diagnostic purposes and subsequent treatment:

1- Patients who are at imminent risk of life threatening arrhythmia e.g. those with a previously recorded episode of VT

2- Patients who had adverse symptoms or signs during the palpitations.

3- Patients with implanted cardiac devices suspected of malfunction.

4- Patients with a family history of sudden death (eg, Brugada Syndrome).

5- Patients who require admission for investigation or treatment of an underlying cause or precipitating illness, for example acute coronary syndrome, electrolyte disturbance or endocrine disorder.

- Patients for whom admission is not necessary will fall into two groups:

1- Those for whom an innocent diagnosis is confidently achieved (either cardiac or non-cardiac)

2- Those whose symptoms have resolved and in whom no specific aetiology has been demonstrated and they have none of the admission criteria above.

- Is further investigation required if a diagnosis is not made?

Patients with a suspected arrhythmia (eg. pre-excitation on their ECG) or structural heart disease (eg. a murmur on auscultation) but without high risk features mandating admission will require referral to cardiology for follow-up, further investigation and management. While awaiting the clinic appointment these patients will benefit from referral for ambulatory monitoring +/- echocadiography

- Advice on Discharge:

Patients should avoid stimulants such as caffeine, alcohol and nicotine. It is useful to keep a record of episodes and any associated symptoms. If the palpitations recur patients should attend the ED if they are persistent or are associated with adverse features.

Chapter 16

Collapse, dizziness and fall history taking approach

The general approach

Put in your mind while interviewing patient presented with history of dizziness or collapse that you are looking for one or combination of syncope/presyncope, seizure, vertigo or fall. Vertigo could be confused or combined with syncope/presyncope. Fall could be simple mechanical or more confusing resulted from syncope, vertigo or seizure; so the most important thing here is to know what exactly ongoing.

Introduction:
As described earlier in chapter 12

Presenting complaint:
As described earlier in chapter 11 but beware that defining the nature of the complaint in this station is the most challenging part, so take your time to ask again and summarize back to the patient:
* What do you remember of the event if any?
* Any dizziness? What do you mean by dizziness? Spinning sensation/vertigo? Disequilibrium/imbalance when standing or walking? Fatigue/general weakness? Light-headedness/going to faint/pre-syncope?
* Any fall? Is it mechanical fall?
* Any blackout/fainting/syncope?
* Any shaking movements?
* Offer anti-sickness tablet

History of presenting complaint:
Event:
Any witness?
Event details:
* ODPARA: as described earlier in chapter 11:
1- Onset:
- Sudden → seizure and vertigo (peripheral and vertbrobasilar insufficiency)
- Gradual → syncope and most of central vertigo
2- Duration and Progression:
- Seconds → syncope especially arrhythmias, peripheral vertigo or vertbrobasilar insufficiency
- Minutes → peripheral vertigo, vertebrobasilar insufficiency or seizures
- Hours or days – intermittent → peripheral vertigo
- Weeks or months – continuous → most of central vertigo
3- Aggravating and Relieving factors:
Will be discussed later in pre-event section

4- Associations:
- Nausea and vomiting: severe in peripheral vertigo and mild in central vertigo
- Neurological symptoms: headache, limb numbness/weakness or speech disturbances → central vertigo
- Auditory symptoms: blocked/buzzing ears or hearing loss → peripheral vertigo
* In case of loss of consciousness ask about:
1- Color of lips:
- Pale → syncope
- Cyanosed → seizure
2- Shaking movements:
- After loss of consciousness → syncope
- Tonic colonic movement, automatism or neck turned to one side → seizure
3- Tongue biting:
- On the tip → syncope
- On the side → seizure
4- Urine incontinence:
In seizures
Pre-event:
Are you pregnant?
* Ectopic → syncope/presyncope (orthostatic hypotension)
* Eclampsia → seizure
Any recent illness or trauma?
* Dehydration or bleeding → syncope/presyncope (orthostatic hypotension) or fatigue due to anemia
* Electrolytes imbalance (?Addison's or GE) → hyperkalamia can cause arrhythmias and hyponatraemia can cause seizures
* URTI → peripheral vertigo or fatigue due to viral illness
* Head injury or high fever → seizure
What did you do before it?
* Posture/position: prolonged standing/orthostatic stress (vasovagal attack) or supine (cardiovascular syncope/presyncope)
* Provoking factors (activity):
1- Emotional stress, heat exposure or fatigue → vasovagal attack
2- Situational stress (micturition, straining, coughing or pain) → situational syncope/presyncope
3- Neck hair shaving or carotid sinus massage → carotid sinus syncope/presyncope
4- Change in posture from sitting to standing position → orthostatic hypotension
5- Exertion or while supine → cardiovascular syncope/presyncope
6- Neck extension → vertibrobasilar insufficiency (central vertigo)
7- Head movement → peripheral vertigo (single critical position) vs. central vertigo (more than one position)
8- Watching TV or being in noisy environment → seizure
9- Drinking alcohol or injecting drugs → seizure

Any symptoms preceded it?
* Prodrome: vasovagal attack might preceded by nausea, sweating and pallor
* Palpitation, SOB or chest pain → cardiovascular syncope/presyncope or PE
* Aura: seizure attack might preceded by unpleasant smell or epigasrtic pain
Post event:
* Rapid recovery with nausea or vomiting afterwards → syncope
* Confusion with lost memory of events, muscle aches, joint dislocation and might sustained other injuries → seizure
Any previous similar episodes?

Past medical, surgical history and hospitalization:
* Cardiac problems as described earlier in chapter 12 and 15 → cardiovascular syncope
* Diabetes, diabetic neuropathy and parkinsonism → orthostatic hypotension or disequilibrium
* Neck arthritis → vertigo
* Ear problems → vertigo
* Neurological problems → headache, seizure or stroke → vertigo and seizures
* Surgery: cardiovascular (balloon, CABG, Valve or carotid), ears or brain

MAFTOS (Medications, Allergies, Family history, Travel history, Social history):
Medications and allergies:
* Antihypertensive and cardiac medications → orthostatic hypotension or cardiovascular syncope
* Use of insulin can give clue to the possibility of hypoglycaemia as a cause of seizure
* Use of steroids can give clue to the possibility of Addison's disease as a cause of syncope
* Anti-epileptic medications → seizure
* Any allergy to medicine?
Family history:
* Cardiac: as described earlier in chapter 12 and 15 with concentration on family history of cardiac valve disease or rhythm disturbances
* Neurological: epilepsy
Social history:
As described earlier in chapter 12 but beware that:
* Alcohol excess or withdrawal can cause seizure or arrhythmias especially AF
* Illicit drugs can cause seizures
In case of seizure you have to discuss:
Issues of occupation, driving, activity of daily living, alcohol and drug abuse

In case of mechanical fall or syncope in elderly you have to discuss:
1- Issues of accommodation (how many floors, stairs – indoors/outdoors and lift)
2- Social support (spouse, partner, family, friends, carers and frequency of their visits)
3- Activity of daily livings (who does the shopping, cooking, washing and cleaning)
4- In addition to occupation, financial issues, alcohol and drug abuse

Closing:

As described earlier in chapter 11

Plan:

Specify plan according to the scenario (Syncope, seizure, vertigo or fall), but generally the following plan will be suitable for most cases:

* Vital signs and postural blood pressure measurement: >20mmgh drop in SBP or >10mmgh in DBP within 3 minutes of standing is the classic evidence of orthostatic hypotension
* Examination: general (pallor → bleeding, dehydration, rash → infection/seizure), cardiovascular, neurological and cerebellar, ear, head movement and rectal examination (? Bleeding)
* Urine: for evidence of dehydration (orthostatic hypotension), pregnancy (ectopic and eclampsia) or urine infection (situational syncope)
* Blood: blood glucose, electrolytes, CBC and Bhcg
* ECG: presence of any of the following changes points clearly to cardiovascular syncope (persistent sinus bradycardia, sinus pause >3 seconds, mobitz II, Complete Heart Block, trifascicular block, alternating RBBB&LBBB, tachyarrhythmia, torsades, long or short QT or Brugada syndrome)
* CXR: look for chest infection

Examples from previous exams

Syncope

DD:

Reflex syncope	Orthostatic hypotension	Cardiovascular syncope
* Vasovagal syncope * Situational syncope * Carotid sinus syncope	* Dehydration, GI or internal bleeding * DM or Parkinson's disease	* Arrhythmias * Structural heart disease * Cardiovascular collapse – PE or AD

Plan:

Depends on the cause, for example:

Cardiovascular syncope:

For example brugada syndrome → put the patient on cardiac monitor in resuscitation room then refer to cardiology for ICD (Implantable Cardioverter Defibrillator)

Situational syncope:

For example syncope on straining in micturition in elderly patient on multiple antihypertensive and cardiac medications → reassure, review medications, urine dipstick for possible UTI, social circumstances discussion and GP follow up

Seizure

DD:

Previous history of epilepsy	No history of epilepsy
* Drug non-compliance	* Drug withdrawal syndromes
* Drug withdrawal	(alcohol, barbiturates or
* Drug therapy change	benzodiazepines)
* Inter-current illness	* Acute structural brain injury
* Metabolic abnormalities	(stroke, SAH, trauma or cerebral
* Drug interactions (co-ingestion	hypoxia)
of drugs that lower the seizure	* CNS infection (meningitis,
threshold)	encephalitis or abscess)
	* Drug overdose (TCAs)

Plan:

Depends on the cause, for example in first fit scenario:

* If examination and investigations are normal patient will go home with follow up in first fit clinic within 2 weeks but before discharge give patient or relative the following advice verbally and in written:

1- How to recognize seizure

2- First aid advice on how to manage a subsequent seizure

3- Safety advice: not locking bathroom doors, swimming unsupervised or operation of heavy machinery

4- Driving advice: the patient can't drive for 6 months extended to 1 year if diagnosed with epilepsy and he must inform the DVLA (Driver and Vehicle Licensing Agency)

* If there is any abnormalities in examination or investigations you will need additional tests (? head scan) or stay in the hospital

Vertigo

DD:

Peripheral:
BPPV (Benign Paroxysmal Positional Vertigo), menier's disease, vestibular neuritis, acute labrynthitis, otitis media, cholesteatoma or acoustic neuroma

Central:
Stroke/TIA, vertebrobasilar or brain stem ischemia, vertebral artery dissection, space occupying lesion, migraine, focal seizure or multiple sclerosis

Plan:
Depends on the cause, for example in case of peripheral vertigo:
* We will give you prochlorperazine and IV fluids; if examination and investigations are normal and you are symptoms free you will go home with ENT doctor follow up for more tests/work up
* If there is any abnormalities in examination or investigations or still symptomatic you will need additional tests (? head scan) or stay in the hospital

Fall

DD:
* Intrinsic factors:
1- Gait and musculoskeletal dysfunction
2- Foot problems
3- Cognitive or other neurological impairment
4- Cardiovascular disease or other acute illness like infection
* Extrinsic factors:
1- Environmental hazards
2- Polypharmacy
3- Use of walking stick or frame
4- Prior history of fall

Plan:
* Identify the serious causes
* Address the social issues
* Disposition depends on the cause; for example if you suspect an arrhythmias behind the fall you have to admit but if you suspect that the cause of fall is mechanical fall or simple slip associated with polypharmacy and aging then you can discharge the patient with fall clinic follow up

Chapter 17

Headache history taking approach

Introduction:
As described earlier in chapter 12
Presenting complaint:
* As described in chapter 11
* Any medicines tried at home? What? When? Did it help?
History of presenting complaint:
Event:
* ODPARA: as described earlier in chapter 1
* SOCRATES: as described earlier in chapter 11
* Associations:
- General: any nausea, vomiting, fever, rash, dizziness or URTI symptoms?
- Neurological: any numbness, weakness, speech disturbances, syncope, seizures or confusion?
- Meningococcal disease: neck pain or photophobia
- Ear symptoms: any ear pain, hearing loss or ear discharge?
- Sinus symptoms: any facial pain or thick yellow nasal discharge?
- Visual symptoms: any recent change in vision? Or eye pain? → Errors of refractions or glaucoma
- Cluster: any conjunctival injection, lacrimation, nasal congestion or rhinorrhoea?
- Temporal arteritis: any weight loss, night sweating, jaw claudication, shoulder stiffness, muscle aches or reduced vision?
Pre-event:
Are you pregnant?
Pre-eclampsia
Any recent illness or trauma? Any contact with ill patient?
URTI or head trauma
What did you do before it?
* Posture/position: if headache came on bending position this may be sinusitis or increased intracranial pressure (ICP).
* Provoking factors (activity):
 - Sex: SAH or post-coital headache
- Sleeping → awake patient from sleep → cluster headache
- Coughing/straining → sinusitis or increased ICP
- Chewing or touch face or scalp → trigeminal neuralgia.
Any symptoms preceded it?
* Prodrome → aura → unpleasant smell and epigastric sensation → migraine
Any previous similar episodes?

Past medical, surgical history and hospitalization:
* Hypertension
* Headaches: migraine (frequency and triggers), tension or cluster
* ENT or Visual problems
* Neck arthritis
* Surgery: ENT, eye or intracranial

MAFTOS (Medications, Allergies, Family history, Travel history, Social history):

Medications and allergies:
* Antihypertensive
* Seldinafil
* Anticoagulants (blood thinners)
* Oral contraceptive pills → migraine
* Any use of over the counter medicines? Any abrupt withdrawal of use?
* Any allergy to medicine?

Family history:
Any illnesses run in the family or suffered by parents like hypertension, migraine, cluster headache, epilepsy or malignancy?

Social history:
As described earlier in chapter 12 but beware that alcohol may precipitate cluster headache and that cocaine and marijuana can cause SAH

Closing:
As described earlier in chapter 11, beware of:

DD:
* Common: tension, migraine and cluster
* Uncommon but important: SAH, trigeminal neuralgia, temporal arteritis and meningitis
* Unilateral: Trigeminal neuralgia, cluster, temporal arteritis and migraine
* Occipital: SAH, meningitis, occipital migraine, occipital neuralgia and post coital headache

Examples from previous exams:
* Trigeminal neuralgia: stabbing unilateral pain within the distribution of the trigeminal nerve and stimulation of the trigger area by touching, hair brushing or chewing induces very severe pain
* Cluster headache: usually occur at night waking the patient, sometimes alcohol may act as precipitant, headaches are typically clustered into up to 8 attacks per day each lasting between 15-180 minute, pain is usually severe and centered upon the eye, associated symptoms are usually unilateral and includes: lacrimation, rhinorrhoea, sweating, ptosis and miosis and often there is positive family history.

* SAH: sudden, worst ever, may be post coital and usually there is past history of previous similar less severe attack.

Plan:

* Vital signs: blood pressure
* Examination: neurological, neck, scalp for tenderness (temporal arteritis or occipitofrontalis muscle spasm) and fundoscopy (high ICP)
* Blood tests including ESR (for temporal arteritis)
* High flow oxygen for 15min (for cluster headache)
* Medications: paracetamol, NSAIDs and metoclopramide (carbamzepine for trigeminal neuralgia)
* Head scan if indicated (trauma, features of increased ICP, sudden worst ever headache or sudden new onset/new pattern headache → have low threshold in patients on anticoagulation)
* LP: for suspected meningitis or (SAH with normal CT brain → 12 hours from onset of headache and look for xanthochromia)
* Special consideration in the case of trigeminal neuralgia:
- If normal examination, investigations and pain free → prescribe carbamazepine and GP follow up with return back instructions
- If there is any abnormality in examination, investigations or still in pain → you may need additional tests or stay in the hospital (looking for secondary causes of trigeminal neuralgia like tumor, aneurysm, multiple sclerosis or herpes zoster)

Chapter 18

Gastrointestinal history taking approach

The general approach

Introduction:
As described earlier in chapter 12 but ask about recent job change or recent stress

Presenting complaint:
As described earlier in chapter 11 but offer anti-sickness tablets if appropriate and ensure that the patient is stable if presented with bleeding or acute abdomen

History of presenting complaint:
* ODPARA: as described earlier in chapter 1
* SOCRATES: as described earlier in chapter 11
* Symptoms suggesting anemia: feeling tired, shortness of breath on exertion or heart racing?
* Systemic upset: fever, malaise, feeling sick or being sick
* Pain: any epigastric pain? Any lower tummy pain? Any back passage pain?
* Bleeding: any bleeding per rectum? Any vomiting of blood? Any blood in urine? Any blood from nose or mouth? Any cough of blood? Any bleeding in the skin? Any heavy menses?
* Cancer: any recent loss of weight, loss of appetite or lumps in your body?
* Any recent trauma?
* Any yellowish discoloration of the skin or eye whites?
* Any difficult or painful swallowing or indigestion?
* Bowel habits: any loose motion or constipation?
* Any rash or joint pain? Inflammatory bowel disease (IBD)
* Any contact with ill patient?
* Any previous similar episodes?

Past medical, surgical history and hospitalization:
* Any previous bowel disease like IBD, irritable bowel syndrome (IBS) or growth?
* Any previous stomach disease like peptic ulcer or growth?
* Any previous gall stones?
* Any previous liver disease or growth? → Bleeding tendency or esophageal varices
* Any previous kidney disease, renal failure or dialysis? → Bleeding tendency
* Any previous heart disease? → Hepatic congestion
* Any blood disease/easy bleeding? → bleeding tendency
* Any previous camera test? From mouth or back passage?

* Any previous surgical operation? → adhesions in case of abdominal pain

MAFTOS (Medications, Allergies, Family history, Travel history, Social history):

Medications and allergies:

* Any regular medicines like aspirin/NSAIDs or steroids?

* Any use of blood thinners?

* Any recent use of antibiotics? → Interaction with blood thinners or of special importance in case of diarrhea

* Any allergy to medicine?

Family history:

Any illnesses run in your family like bowel diseases (IBD, growth or polyps) or jaundice?

Travel history:

Any recent travel? → Delhi belly in case of abdominal pain or diarrhea

Social history:

As described earlier in chapter 12 but beware of:

* Alcohol is related to peptic ulcer or liver disease

* IV drug use is related to viral hepatitis

* Sexual history is important in UTI, STDs or hepatitis scenarios

* Diet: Any recent change in diet?

Closing:

As described earlier in chapter 11; for example:

Plan:

In cases of upper GI bleeding and epigastric/Right Upper Quadrant pain:

* Vital signs

* Abdominal and rectal examination

* Blood tests including liver profile (especially in significant alcohol history)

* Recommend to stop NSAIDs

* Ask the patient if he would like help to reduce alcohol intake

* Offer referral to alcohol liaison team

* Advise for stress management

* Advice for safe diet

* Camera test

* Follow up

Examples from previous exams

GI bleeding

History of presenting complaint:

* Color: What is the color? bright red or dark?

* Quantity: How many times? Over how long? How much? Any clots?

* Pattern: Have you been vomited repeatedly? → Mallory Weiss tear

DD:

Systemic:

Blood disease or use of blood thinners

Local:

Upper:

* Esophagus: Esophageal varices due to alcoholic liver disease and mallory Weiss tear
* Stomach: Peptic ulcer disease (PUD)
* Both: Cancer and erosions

Lower:

* Bowel: infective, tumor (benign or malignant), trauma, IBD (ulcerative colitis, crhon's disease or diverticular disease) and angiodysplasia
* Ano-rectal: piles, fissure and trauma

Plan:

Tailor the plan according to the presentation and the scenario; in case of haematemesis for example apply the clinical rockall score:

score	0	1	2	3
Age	<60	60-79	80 or more	
Shock	No shock (HR<100, SBP>100)	Tachycardia (HR>100, SBP>100)	Hypotension (HR>100, SBP<100)	
Co-morbidity	No major co-morbidity		Cardiac failure, IHD, any major co-morbidity)	Renal failure, liver failure, disseminated malignancy

Score 0: discharge with clinic follow

Score 0-3 (low risk): urgent camera test as outpatient

Score >3 (high risk): ITU admission and emergency endoscopy

Abdominal pain

DD:

For example:

RUQ (Right Upper Quadrant) pain:

* Acute cholecystitis or biliary colic
* Duodenal ulcer
* Hepatitis
* Congestive hepatomegaly
* Pyelonephritis
* Appendicitis
* Right basal pneumonia

LLQ (Left Lower Quadrant) pain:
* Sigmoid diverticulitis
* Salpingitis
* Tubo-ovarian abscess
* Ruptured ectopic pregnancy
* Incarcerated hernia
* Perforated colon
* Crhon's disease or Ulcerative colitis
* Renal or ureteric stone

Plan:
Tailor the plan according to the scenario and the findings in the history taking, but generally the following tests will be helpful:
Urine dipstick
Pregnancy test
Imaging:
* Chest X ray erect position to look for bowel perforation either from PUD or IBD
* US abdomen and pelvis
In case of RUQ pain:
* Acute cholecystitis: antibiotics and surgical referral
* Biliary colic/chronic cholecystitis: if the patient is pain free with normal examination and blood tests then he could be discharged home with outpatient US and follow up
* Obstructive jaundice: mostly will need admission for more work up especially if the gall bladder is palpable in examination so CA pancreas is likely
* Ascending cholangitis: triad of pain, fever and jaundice will need admission for sepsis management
In cased of LLQ pain:
* CT abdomen
* Plain X ray abdomen: look for bowel obstruction or toxic mega colon (if bowel loop dilated >5.5cm)
* Acute diverticulitis: antibiotics and surgical referral
* Severe acute colitis: triad of >6 loose bloody motions per day, systemic signs and hypoalbuminaemia will need medical and surgical team referral

Chapter 19

Travel history taking approach

The general approach

Introduction:
As described in chapter 12

Presenting complaint:
* As described earlier in chapter 18 but beware that a patient with fever >38 who visited Ebola area in past 21 days will need immediate isolation in a side room and all staff who will contact with him need to wear full PPE
* Most presenting complaints of the returning travelers are fever and diarrhea

History of presenting complaint:
As described in chapter 18 but beware of adding:
* Pain: Myalgia/Headache →? Malaria/Ebola or tummy/back passage pain → ? Infective diarrhea
* Any contact with ill patient? In case of suspected Ebola infection ask about contact with confirmed or suspected Ebola case or involvement in high risk activities like participation in funerals for Ebola cases
* Anybody else with you ill as well?
* Any history of chronic cough or recurrent infections? → Suspect malignancy, TB or AIDS

Past medical, surgical history and hospitalization:
As described earlier in chapter 18 but beware of adding:
* Any previous exposure to tropical illnesses like malaria, typhoid, Ebola or hepatitis A?
* Any diabetes, IHD, PVD or CHF → ischemic colitis in case of diarrhea
* Any thyroid disease? → In case of diarrhea
* Any recent hospitalization? → In case of infective diarrhea

MAFTOS (Medications, Allergies, Family history, Travel history, Social history):
As described earlier in chapter 18 but add:
Travel history:
* Where? Malaria area? Ebola area (West Africa → Siraleon, Guinea or Liberia)?
* When went and returned?
* When symptoms started? Any illness there? If no illness there, how soon after arriving did symptoms start?
* Any malaria prophylaxis given before travel?
* Any pre-travel vaccination received?
* What did you do there? Work? Holiday?

* Any high risk activities there (participation in funerals of Ebola case or unprotected sex)?
* What type of accommodation used?
* Any use of mosquitoes nets, repellents and long clothing? Any mosquitoes bites over there?
* Any consumption of salad, ice or sea foods over there?

Closing:
As described earlier in chapter 11

Examples from previous exams

Bloody diarrhea

History of presenting complaint:
* Color: What is the color? Red fresh, dark black tarry or streaks of bright red blood in motion?
* Quantity: How many times? Over how long? How much? Any clots?
* Any associated mucus, pus or alternating with constipation?

DD:
* Infective diarrhea: viral, bacterial or protozoal
* Bowel disease: IBD and ischemic colitis
* Antibiotics related

Plan:
* Vital signs
* General examination: lack of body fluids or pale
* Tummy and rectal examination
* Stool culture and microscopy
* Blood tests: CBC, coagulation profile, chemistry and electrolytes
* Oral rehydration or IV fluids if dehydrated
* Antibiotics → ciprofloxacin 500mg PO BD for 5 days: indicated in bloody diarrhea associated with foreign travel, systemic upset, prolonged illness or positive culture/microscopy
* Anti-diarrheal medicine: not recommended
* Hand hygiene advice
* Return work after negative culture
* follow up with GP
* Advice regarding return back instructions
* Written instructions
* Admission if indicated: persistent vomiting or severe dehydration with or without shock

Febrile traveler

DD:
* Viral illness: viral hemorrhagic fever, H1N1 or corona
* Pneumonia
* Gastroenteritis, typhoid fever or hepatitis
* HIV seroconversion
* Malaria or Ebola

Plan:

Vital signs

Examination

Blood test

Partial septic work up:

Blood cultures, urine cultures and CXR

Discuss with ID (Infectious Disease) on call and probably admit

For malaria:

* 3 blood films (thin and thick) over 48-72 hours and antigen tests for malaria
* Beware that parasitaemia 2% means severe falciparum malaria which is liable for complications (cerebral malaria, severe anemia, renal failure, hypoglycemia, DIC, pulmonary edema, pneumonia, acidosis and raised lactate >5)
* Treatment: Quinine IV/oral for falciparum malaria or Chloroquine oral for other types

For Ebola:

* Isolation if not already done
* PPE for all staff taking care of the patient
* Ebola test
* Register all staff or patients contacted with the patient
* Explain nature of the disease to the patient: it is infectious and generally fatal disease marked by fever and severe internal bleeding and spread through contact with infected body fluids by Ebola virus whose normal host is unknown
* Leaflets

Chapter 20

Urology history taking approach

The general approach

Introduction:
* As described earlier in chapter 12
* Beware of importance of asking about the current and previous job; patient with history of working in dye industry or chemicals might have a risk for cancer bladder

Presenting complaint:
As described earlier in chapter 11

In case of renal colic:
* Any medicines tried at home? What? When? Did it help?
* Any allergies to medicines?
* Give diclofenac 100mg rectally then reassess pain after 30-60 minutes
* Give opiates if pain returns or if NSAIDs are contraindicated; morphine 5-10mg SC/IM
* Give cyclizine 50mg oral or parenetral if there is nausea or vomiting

In case of scrotal pain and haematuria if STDs are a possibility:
Pay attention to assure the patient regarding privacy and confidentiality of the information that he will provide and prepare him to the sensitive nature of the sexual history questions

History of presenting complaint:
As described earlier in chapter 18 but beware of:
* Pain: Beside asking about tummy and back passage pain ask about front passage pain/burning micturition, flank pain and balls pain (scrotal pain)
* Genital symptoms: urethral discharge and lumps in the groins
* Presence of rash, eye or joint pains may be a clue for a possibility of STDs as a cause of haematuria or scrotal pain

Past medical, surgical history and hospitalization:
As usual but you can classify it as following to remember it:

General:
* DM and HTN
* Blood disease in case of haematuria
* Gout, hyperparathyroidism and bowel disease are possible risks for stone formation

Local:
* UTI especially if recurrent
* Stones especially if recurrent
* Prostate enlargement
* Polycystic kidney disease, single or transplanted kidney
* Undescended testis or torsion

* Hernia

Interventions:

* Surgery

* Stone treatment with shock waves (ESWL)

* Camera test

* Catheterization or instrumentation

MAFTOS (Medications, Allergies, Family history, Travel history, Social history):

Medications and allergies:

* Specifically ask about use of blood thinners, nephrotoxines and rifampicin in case of haematuria

* Ask about use of metformin (contrast/dye risk) and previous contrast allergy if you might request IVU (Intra Venous Urography)

Family history:

Ask about family history of stone formation

Travel history:

Ask about risk of schistosomiasis in case of haematuria

Social history:

As described earlier in chapter 12 but add:

Sexual history

Diet history:

* Reduced liquids intake in case of renal colic

* Ingestion of beetroot and berries in case of haematuria (factitious)

Closing:

As described earlier in chapter 11

Plan:

* Vital signs

* Examination:

- General: look for signs of dehydration, infection and uremia

- Local: abdomen&renal angle (look for tenderness or mass), bladder (look for retention or mass), groin (look for lymphadenopathy or hernia) and rectal (look for enlarged prostate)

* Urine dipstick:

Look for blood, nitrite or leucocytes

* Blood tests:

- Basic screens and CBC will usually required

- Coagulation profile and type&screen will be required in case of haematuria

- PSA (Prostate Specific Antigen) may be required in case of enlarged prostate

* Imaging:

- IVU or CT KUB in case of renal colic

- Abdomen US with comment on Post Void Residual Volume (PVR) in case of enlarged prostate

Examples from previous exams

Renal colic

DD:
* Appendicitis, cholecystitis, pyelonephritis
* AAA (Abdominal Aortic Aneurysm)
* Ovarian pathology or ectopic pregnancy
* Testicular torsion
* Musculoskeletal pain

Plan:
* Discharge for imaging within 48 hours with clinic follow up if:
- Pain free
- No renal impairment
- No obstruction: no urine retention clinically and no back pressure by bedside US
* Admission if:
- Systemically unwell with fever
- Persistent pain
- Persistent nausea and vomiting especially if dehydrated
- Single transplanted kidney
- Bilateral obstructing stones
 - Diagnostic uncertainty
- Acute kidney injury or hydronephrosis
* Definitive treatment:
- Camera test: ureteroscopy
- ESWL (Shock waves)

Enlarged prostate

History of presenting complaint:
* Are you going to toilet more frequently?
* How many times did you get up to urinate at night?
* Have you found it difficult to postpone urination? How often?
* Any strain to begin urination? How often?
* Any weak urinary stream? How often?
* Have you found you stopped and started again several times when you urinated? How often?
* Any sensation of not emptying your bladder completely? How often?
* Any urge to urinate again less than two hours after finished urination? How often?

Social history:
* Any impact on ADLs?
* How would you consider treatment successful?
* Would you consider treatment successful if you could return to normal activity?
DD:
BPH and CA prostate
Plan:
We are going to do blood test called PSA (Prostate Specific Antigen); if it is positive we will proceed to further tests but if it is negative you will have the choice either to try medicine or to undergo a surgery and in both cases you have to manage your liquids intake and avoid caffeine.
Medications: Tamsulosin – alpha blocker
* Check blood pressure before use, avoid if the patient is prone to postural hypotension and to avoid hypotension start at low dose
* Common side effects: dizziness
* Unusual side effects: drowsiness, weakness and dry mouth
Surgery: TURB – Trans Urethral Resection of Prostate:
* Effective but reserved to severe symptoms not responding to medications
* Complications: incontinence and impotence

Haematuria

History of presenting complaint:
* Color: bright red or dark?
* Quantity: how many times? How much? Any clots?
DD:
Systemic:
* Blood disease
* Anticoagulant use
* Exercise
* Factitious (rifampicine, beetroot or berries)
Local:
* Infection (UTI)
* Growth (CA bladder or renal cell carcinoma)
* Stone
* Prostate (enlargement or infection)
* Trauma (catheterization and instrumentation)
* Stricture
* Glomerulonephritis
* AAA
Plan:
Most of cases will be discharged with clinic follow up for further tests but you might admit some cases as:
* Clot retention: for three way catheter till urine become clear
* Coagulation defect: for correction

Scrotal pain

History of presenting complaint:
Ask about risk factors for torsion: vigorous sexual activity, trauma, exercise or history of undescended tests

DD:
* Testicular torsion
* Infection: epididymo-orchitis
* Trauma
* Hernia: incarcerated inguinal hernia

Plan:
Testicular torsion:
Urology referral for emergency operative detorsion and try manual detorsion (use nitrous oxide as analgesia)

Epididymo-orchitis:
* Urinalysis and urine culture
* Urethral swab if there is urethral discharge
* Antibiotics
* STDs/HIV tests with follow up in GUM (Genito Urinary Medicine) clinic and contact tracing if the patient is sexually active

Chapter 21

Vaginal bleeding history taking approach

The general approach

Setting:
* Confidential room
* Close mobile and bleep
* Chaperone

Introduction:
* As described earlier in chapter 12

Presenting complaint:
As described earlier in chapter 11 but furthermore ensure stability and assure the patient regarding privacy of information she will give

History of presenting complaint:
* ODPARA: as described earlier in chapter 1
* SOCRATES: as described earlier in chapter 11
* Color: what is the color? bright red or dark?
* Quantity: How many times? Over how long? How much? How many pads changed today? Any clots?
* If the patient's age is in child bearing period it is worth to ask her if she is pregnant or not? If she is pregnant you have to add an important question here; any tissues or fetal parts passed through down passage?
* Symptoms suggesting anemia: Feeling tired, any shortness of breath on exertion or any heart racing?
* Systemic upset: any fever, malaise, feeling sick or being sick
* Pain: ask about tummy, back passage and front passage pain as well as down passage pain?
* Bleeding elsewhere: any bleeding per rectum? Any vomiting of blood? Any blood in urine? Any blood from nose or mouth? Any cough of blood? Any bleeding in the skin?
* Cancer: any recent loss of weight, loss of appetite or lumps in your body?
* Any recent trauma?
* Genital symptoms: vaginal discharge (when did it start? Does it smell? What does it look like? Is it blood stained?) and lumps in the groin → STDs or PID
* Urinary symptoms → STDs
* Any rash, eye, joint pains or red eye? → STDs
* Any previous similar episodes?

Past medical, surgical history and hospitalization:
* Blood and thyroid diseases may contribute to menstrual abnormalities and bleeding episodes
* Presence of breast cancer may give clue for the possibility of presence of concomitant gynecological cancer
* Ask about previous surgery/intervention especially gynecological

MAFTOS (Medications, Allergies, Family history, Travel history, Social history):

Medications and allergies:
* Asking about use of blood thinners is important in this presentation
* Use of tamoxifen affect the plan in case of post-menopausal bleeding → see later
* Use of HRT (Hormone Replacement Therapy) is a risk factor for gynecological growths

Social history:
As usual but beware of the importance of sexual history:
* warn the patient regarding the personal nature of the questions
* Clarify that answer to these questions are important for diagnosis
* You will have little time to ask about full sexual history so at least ask quickly 3 questions for which the answer likely to be negative:
1- Any bleeding around time of sex?
2- Any pain around time of sex?
3- Any trauma around time of sex? Any vigorous sex? Any use of sex instruments?

Gynecological history:
* When did you start menstruating?
* When was your LMP (Last Menstrual Period)? Did you have any period abnormalities?
* What age did you go through menopause? (in case of post-menopausal bleeding)
* Last smear/swab: when? What was the result? Did you receive any treatment? What treatment did you receive? Did you receive all the treatment course? Have you had ever an abnormal smear/swab?
* Any previous gynaecological problem? STDs, PID or fibroids?

Pregnancy history:
If the patient is pregnant don't forget to ask:
* G? P? A? How many weeks pregnant?
* Any follow up, blood tests or scans during this pregnancy?
* Any previous problems in this pregnancy or other pregnancies?
* Ask about the nature of pregnancy? Is it IVF (In Vitro Fertilisation) pregnancy? Where performed? Any previous IVF pregnancy?

Closing:
As described earlier in chapter 11

Examples from previous exams

Post menopausal bleeding

DD:
* Growth (either benign or malignant):
- External genitalia
- Neck of womb
- Womb
* Vaginal atrophy: thinning of wall of vagina
* Lack of hormones
* Blood disease
* Thyroid disease
* Trauma

Plan:
Telling somebody that she might have growth is not an easy job so follow briefly the SPIKES protocol for breaking bad news:

Strategy:
* Vital signs
* Examination: pelvic examination and obtaining smear/swab
* Blood tests: CBC, chemistry and coagulation profile
* Outpatient transvaginal scan and gynecology for all dischargeable stable cases except who is on tamoxifen who require camera test and biopsy instead of transvaginal scan

Miscarriage in a lady

Plan:
This is a common exam case who presented with significant bleeding with clots, tissues and fetal parts and again telling a lady that she might lost her baby is not an easy job especially if it is a precious pregnancy; so again briefly follow the SPIKES protocol for breaking bad news:

Perception:
Establishes what already known and explain the situation; this means that you have to ask the patient about her ideas, concerns and expectations then to brief back the events to her concentrating on the fact of significant bleeding and presence of fetal parts and tissues

Invitation:
Do you want a friend, family member or the father of the baby to be contacted now?

Knowledge:
Tell her that you have bad news for her then say clearly that she probably lost her baby then pause for 10 seconds

Empathy:
As described earlier in chapter 6

Strategy:

* Respond to her enquires; for example tell her that the most likely reason for losing her baby is chromosomal abnormalities

* Tell her what you will do now:

- Vital signs

- Examination: pelvic examination to see if the neck of womb opened or closed and speculum examination to remove any tissue which might be in the neck of the womb

- Tissues and fetal parts will be sent for analysis

- Blood test: CBC and coagulation profile

- Scan: to confirm diagnosis and to look for any retained products

- Gynaecology doctor referral: as you might need further treatment/intervention if there is retained products

- Miscarriage counselling group referral

Chapter 22

Sexual history taking approach

Introduction:
As described earlier in chapter 12
Presenting complaint:
* As described earlier in chapter 11 but beware of assuring the patient regarding privacy and confidentiality of the provided information
* The presenting complaint is usually dysuria, urethral or vaginal discharge or joint pain/swelling; but sometimes the patient present only because he/she did a mistake (for example casual unprotected sex) and want to check that everything is ok
History of presenting complaint:
* ODPARA: as described earlier in chapter 1
* SOCRATES: as described earlier in chapter 11
* Systemic upset: any fever, malaise, feeling sick or being sick
* Pain: ask about tummy pain, back passage pain, front passage pain/burning micturition, flank pain and balls (scrotal) or penis pain
* Genital symptoms:
- Urethral or vaginal discharge (colour and odour)
- Lumps in the groins
- Dysparunia: superficial or deep? During intercourse or ejaculation?
* Urinary symptoms: dysuria, frequency and haematuria
* Bowel symptoms: any change in bowel habits? Any loose motion or constipation?
* Any rash, blisters, ulcers, sores, eye or joint pains or red eyes
* Bleeding: urethral or vaginal
* Any previous similar episodes?
* Any previous joint problems?
Past medical, surgical history and hospitalization:
Especially ask about past history of UTIs or STDs
MAFTOS (Medications, Allergies, Family history, Travel history, Social history):
Medications and allergies:
As usual but beware of hepatitis immunization status
Travel history:
Any unprotected sex while abroad
Social history:
* As usual but take detailed sexual history and before asking the questions prepare the patient for the special nature of the questions:
- Warn the patient about the intimate/personal nature of the questions and reassure regarding confidentiality
- Tell the patient that her/his answers will help you to assess the risk for STDs/HIV infection and the sites to take swabs from

* Follow the following approach:
- Do you have partner? Male or female partner? Since when?
- Do you have another partner or partners?
- Any symptoms in partner/s?
- Any relation of appearance of symptoms to last sexual intercourse?
- Do you always/sometimes/never use condom?
- Any use of contraception (birth control method)? What?
- Do you have previous STDs? What? Any treatment? What was the treatment? Did you take all the treatment course? Any treatment for the partner?
* If there is a specific event that the patient want to talk about then ask the following questions:
Tell me what happened? When that happened? Was it consensual? Was it under effect of drugs or alcohol? Do you have intercourse? Penetrative intercourse? I mean vaginal, anal or oral? Do you know him/her? Where is she/he from? Africa or far east? Did you pay to him/her? Is he/she sex worker? Did you/he used a condom?
* Ask about Blood Born Virus (BBV) risks other than sex → details in chapter 23

Gynecological history:
* When did you start menstruating?
* When was your LMP? Did you have any periods abnormalities?
* Any bleeding between menses? Any bleeding around the time of sex?
* Last smear/swab: when? What was the result? Did you receive any treatment? What treatment did you receive? Did you receive all the treatment course? Have you had ever an abnormal smear/swab?
* Any previous gynaecological problem? STDs, PID, fibroids ... etc?

Closing:
As described earlier in chapter 11 but beware of:

Diagnosis:
* Tell the patient that you are worried of STDs with potential HIV risk, if the history is suggestive
* There is a common station in which a man will present with painful/swollen knee with history suggestive of STDs; in this case tell the patient the same previous statement and add to it that he might have infection in his knee (septic arthritis) or more likely he might have infection elsewhere with just knee reaction to this infection (reactive arthritis) and in his case infection is likely to be urinary and/or genital.

Plan:
* Examination: general and local
* Urine dipstick
* Urethral/vaginal swab
* Blood tests including BhCG
* Knee aspiration to rule out septic arthritis in case of painful and swollen knee
* PEPSE (Post Exposure Prophylaxis after Sexual Exposure to HIV): if there is high risk for HIV exposure and you can find more details in chapter 23

* Antibiotics for Reiter's disease (reactive arthritis) or UTI either STAT dose or longer regimes
* Emergency contraception: to be given if pregnancy test is negative after penetrative intercourse, given as 2 tablets once, warn the patient to return back to receive another dose if she vomited within 3 hours, warn the patient to seek emergency advice if she developed abdominal pain in next two months, advise the patient that the timing of the next period will change, that there is 1 % failure rate and tell the patient to go to her GP to repeat pregnancy test after 2 weeks.
* GUM clinic follow up for STDs screen and HIV test
* Use condom till negative tests
* Advise the patient regarding partner/s disclosure if the tests are positive
* Contact tracing for sexual partner/s

Chapter 23

Percutaeous injury assessment approach

The general approach

Introduction:
As described earlier in chapter 12
Presenting complaint:
* In previous exams this topic appeared as 4 scenarios:
1- Needle-stick injury
2- Mammalian bite
3- Snake bite
4- Rabbit bite
* Play this section as described earlier in chapter 11 but beware of:
- Beside of offering pain killers offer to splint and elevate the limb as part of non-pharmacological treatment of pain except in case of snake bite splint the limb in neutral position
- Check that wound is ok: stop bleeding, irrigate with warm running water and dress bite wounds
History of presenting complaint:
* What happened? Establish that injury was percutaneous
* How?
* Where? In case of hand bites ask about hand dominance
* When? In case of bites antibiotics are given within 72 hours
* Ask whether the injury broken the skin:
- In case of needle stick injury ask whether he/she worn gloves and if there was blood over the needle
- In case of bites ask if it was over bared or clothed skin
* What did you do after injury? Did the wound bleed? Did you encourage bleeding? Did you wash it or clean it with disinfectant?
* Any other injuries?
* Any previous similar injuries?
* Ask about any local symptoms or reactions: pain, swelling or ecchymosis
* Ask about the donor (the patient in case of needle-stick injury and the attacker in case of mammalian bite) or the animal:
- In case of needle stick injury and mammalian bite: do you know the donor?
- In case of snake bite: do you have a picture of the snake?
- In case of other animal injury: is it domestic or wild animal?
* Are you pregnant?
Past medical, surgical history and hospitalization:
Immunosuppressive illness: DM, chronic kidney disease or cancer

MAFTOS (Medications, Allergies, Family history, Travel history, Social history):

Medications and allergies:

* Last tetanus vaccination

* Immunosuppressive medicines: cancer medicines or steroids

Closing:

As described earlier in chapter 11 but beware of bite wound management:

Examination:

* Look at the bite for signs of infections

* Examine the limb for neurovascular or tendon injures

* Look for other injuries elsewhere

X ray:

Indicated for:

- Clenched fist injuries

- Crush injuries

- Possibility of fracture or FB in the wound

- Penetrating scalp injuries

Wound treatment:

- Photograph and swab it

- Soak it with disinfectant

- Plan either exploration under LA or referral to plastic surgery for further management

- Primary closure will be delayed except in two situations:

1- Bite in face: immediate primary closure

2- Bite over MCPJ: refer to orthopedic for exploration and washout in the theatre

- Tetanus vaccination

- Antibiotics: given within 72 hours of bite; for example you can prescribe augmentin for 7 days or a quinolone in case of allergy to penicillin

Examples from previous exams

Needle stick injury and mammalian bite

Actually this is two stations not one but I wrote it as one topic because of the similar specific approach in history taking and management plan

History of presenting complaint:

* Ask more questions about the donor:

- Who is the donor?

- Where is he/she?

- What do you know about him/her?

- What is his/her HIV status?

* If he/she don't know the donor's HIV status:
- tell him/her that you will try to contact the donor to know his/her HIV status
- Ask him/her if he/she knows that the donor has any BBV risks:
1- Use of IV drugs or shared needles
2- Homosexual or bisexual contact
3- Sexual contact with a partner lived in an area of high HIV endemicity or sex worker
4- Has a partner with known HIV
5- History of blood transfusions before 1985 in UK or at any time in developing countries

MAFTOS (Medications, Allergies, Family history, Travel history, Social history):

Medications and allergies:

Hepatitis immune status:

* Unvaccinated
* Vaccinated: ask about the antibody titre level

Social history:

As usual and ask about BBV risks

Plan:

Post Exposure Prophylaxis (PEP) to HIV:

* Explain that risk of HIV transmission in case of percutaneous injury is 3/1000 or 3/100
* Explain that treatment is best given within one hour of exposure
* Seek his/her own views on having PEP
* Explain that drugs prescribed are Truvada 1 tablet OD and Kaletra 2 tablets BD
* Tell the patient that these medicines will be continued for 4 weeks
* Explain that side effects of these medicines are: nausea, vomiting and diarrhoea
* Tell the patient that you will prescribe antiemetic and antidiarrhoeal medicine to avoid the side effects
* Ask the patient to seek medical advice in case of persistent vomiting
* Obtain consent to perform blood test; tell the patient that you will take a baseline blood sample for HIV test now then he/she will need to follow up with GP for further HIV tests at 12 and 24 weeks and you may need to explain why (seroconversion period for HIV)
 * Tell the patient that you will see the feasibility to take blood from the donor for the same purpose
* Advise him/her regarding barrier contraception and to avoid blood donation till the 24 weeks' test is negative
* In case of needle stick injury: report the incident to occupational health department for workplace-related incidents risk assessment and actions
* If the patient gave consent to proceed contact on call PEP specialist
 * Arrange follow up with GP

Snake bite

History of presenting complaint:
Systemic reaction:
* GI: metallic taste, nausea and vomiting
* Neurological: oral numbness, tingling, dizziness and muscle fasciculation
* Hematological: rash and urine discoloration
* Cardiac: heart racing and chest pain
* Respiratory: SOB and oral swelling
Plan:
* Vital signs
* Examination: to confirm presence/absence of local and systemic reactions
* Workup: CBC, chemistry, coagulation profile, fibrinogen and FDA
* Anti-venom and ITU admission if there is progressive swelling, systemic reactions, unstable vital signs or abnormal labs otherwise observe for 8 hours for local and systemic reactions and discharge if symptoms free

Rabbit bite

Plan:
* Contact infectious disease specialist for advice regarding PEP to rabies
* Reassure the patient that PEP to rabies if indicated can be given at even late stage because of long incubation period of the rabies virus (14 to 90 days)

BMA LIBRARY

BRITISH MEDICAL ASSOCIATION

21776202R00060

Printed in Great Britain
by Amazon